THE NEW REALITIES

Books by Peter F. Drucker

MANAGEMENT

The Frontiers of Management
Innovation and Entrepreneurship
The Changing World of the Executive
Managing in Turbulent Times
Management: Tasks, Responsibilities, Practices
Technology, Management and Society
The Effective Executive
Managing for Results
The Practice of Management
Concept of the Corporation

ECONOMICS, POLITICS, SOCIETY

Toward the Next Economics
The Unseen Revolution
Men, Ideas and Politics
The Age of Discontinuity
Landmarks of Tomorrow
America's Next Twenty Years
The New Society
The Future of Industrial Man
The End of Economic Man

FICTION

The Temptation to Do Good
The Last of All Possible Worlds

AUTOBIOGRAPHY

Adventures of a Bystander

PETER F. DRUCKER

THE NEW REALITIES

IN GOVERNMENT AND POLITICS/

IN ECONOMICS AND BUSINESS/

IN SOCIETY AND WORLD VIEW

PERENNIAL LIBRARY

HARPER & ROW, PUBLISHERS, New York

Grand Rapids, Philadelphia, St. Louis, San Francisco

London, Singapore, Sydney, Tokyo, Toronto

A hardcover edition of this book was published in 1989 by Harper & Row, Publishers.

THE NEW REALITIES. Copyright © 1989 by Peter F. Drucker. All rights reserved. Printed in the United States of America. No part of this book may be used or reproduced in any manner whatsoever without written permission except in the case of brief quotations embodied in critical articles and reviews. For information address Harper & Row, Publishers, Inc., 10 East 53rd Street, New York, NY 10022.

First PERENNIAL LIBRARY edition published 1990.

The Library of Congress has catalogued the hardcover edition as follows:

Drucker, Peter Ferdinand, 1909–
    The new realities : in government and politics, in economics and
business, in society and world view / by Peter F.
Drucker.—1st ed.
      p. cm.
    Includes index.
    ISBN 0-06-016129-9
    1. World politics—1985–1995.   2. Economic history—1971–
3. Information society.   I. Title.
D849.D78   1989
909.82—dc19   89-1992

ISBN 0-06-091699-0 (pbk.)
90 91 92 93 94 FG 10 9 8 7 6 5 4 3 2

To my Grandchildren:
Nova, Marin, Jeremy, Miya, Keith, and Allison

CONTENTS

PREFACE

This book is not about "things to come." It is not about the "next century." Its thesis is that the "next century" is already here, indeed that we are well advanced into it. We do not know the answers. But we do know the issues. The courses of action open to us can be discerned. And so can those which, however popular, will be futile, if not counterproductive. The realities are different from the issues on which politicians, economists, scholars, businessmen, union leaders still fix their attention, still write books, still make speeches. The convincing proof of this is the profound sense of unreality that characterizes so much of today's politics and economics. And thus, while this book is not "futurism," it attempts to define the concerns, the issues, the controversies that will be *realities* for years to come.

Some of the toughest problems we face are those created by the successes of the past—the success of the welfare state, for example; the success of this century's invention of the fiscal state; the success of the knowledge society. Some of the greatest impediments to effectiveness are the slogans, the commitments, the issues of yesterday, which still dominate public discourse, still confine our vision. Also, some half-forgotten lessons of the past are becoming relevant again. The nineteenth-century experiences of Austria-Hungary and of the British in India with the impact of economic development on nationalism and colonialism mean a great deal for the future of the Russian Empire, for instance. This explains why a good deal of history is included.

This is an ambitious book that casts its net over a wide range of subjects. Written in the United States by an American, it does not confine itself to American topics; it deals fully as much with government, society, and economy in Japan, in Western Europe, in Russia, and in the Third World of developing countries. Yet the book may also be faulted for not being ambitious enough. The impacts of technology on arms and defense; on the function and limits of government; on schools and learning are frequently discussed. No chapter as such is however devoted to technology per se. This subject, I felt, is abundantly discussed in a spate of works. While highly important, technology is hardly "news" any more.

An even greater limitation: this book deals with the "surface," the "social superstructure"—politics and government, society, economy and economics, social organization and education. The foundations—world view and values and the shifts in both—are mentioned often, but are discussed only in a few short pages at the very end. And there is no discussion of the spiritual agonies and moral horrors: the tyranny and brutal lust for power; the terror and cruelty; the naked cynicism, that have engulfed the world since the West's descent into World War I. For this I lack both authority and competence.

This book does not focus on what to do tomorrow. It

focuses on what to do *today* in contemplation of tomorrow. Within self-imposed limitations, it attempts to set the agenda.

—PETER F. DRUCKER
Claremont, California
Spring 1989

PART I

THE POLITICAL
REALITIES

1

THE DIVIDE

Even in the flattest landscape there are passes where the road first climbs to a peak and then descends into a new valley. Most of these passes are only topography, with little or no difference in climate, language, or culture between the valleys on either side. But some passes are different. They are true divides. They often are neither high nor spectacular. The Brenner is the lowest and gentlest of the passes across the Alps; yet from earliest times it has marked the border between Mediterranean and Nordic cultures. The Delaware Water Gap, some seventy miles west of New York City, is not even a real pass; yet it still divides Eastern seaboard and mid-America.

History, too, knows such divides. They also tend to be unspectacular and are rarely much noticed at the time. But once these divides have been crossed, the social and political landscape changes. Social and political climate is different and so is social and political language. *There are new realities.*

Some time between 1965 and 1973 we passed over such

a divide and entered "the next century." We passed out of creeds, commitments, and alignments that had shaped politics for a century or two. We are in political *terra incognita* with few familiar landmarks to guide us. No one except a mere handful of Stalinists believes any more in salvation by society—the faith which since the eighteenth century's Enlightenment had been the dominant force and main engine of politics. But the one effective political counterforce is also spent: political integration in and through interest blocs. It was America's own contribution to the art and practice of politics, fashioned first by Mark Hanna at the very end of the last century and then perfected, forty years later, by Franklin D. Roosevelt in the New Deal.

The last of the colonial empires, Russia, has entered the final phase of decolonization. Whatever succeeds, it is unlikely to be either "Russian" or "Empire."

And after three hundred or more years in which armaments were "productive" and worked as instruments of policy, they have become "counterproductive": an economic drain if not economically crippling; treacherous as a tool of politics; and—the most important and least expected change—impotent militarily.

These are the main realities to be discussed in this first part of the book.

1873–1973

The last such "divide" was crossed exactly a century earlier, in 1873. In its economic impacts that year's crash on the Vienna Stock Market was a non-event. All it did was to set off short-lived stock market panics in Frankfurt, London, Paris, and New York. Eighteen months later the economy throughout the entire Western world had fully recovered.

But politically the crash on a fairly obscure stock exchange marked the end of the Liberal era, the end of the one hundred years in which laissez-faire was the dominant political creed.

That century had begun in 1776 with the *Wealth of Nations* by Adam Smith. Within ten years after 1873, the great Liberal parties that had marched under the banners of "progress" and "enlightenment" all over the West were in retreat and disarray. They never recovered.

On the European continent they almost immediately split into Marxist and anti-Semitic Socialists. Both were equally anti-capitalist, and hostile to free markets and "bourgeois democracy." Anti-Semitism appealed to the traditional anti-capitalists, the peasants and small tradesmen, rather than to the "post-capitalist" industrial worker. It was however as much rejection of laissez-faire and of the bourgeois ethos as Marxism. And like Marxist socialism, it was defined from the beginning, quite openly, as engine of political integration and as organizing principle for the conquest of political power. In fact, the first politician anywhere to put into effect a Socialist program and to expropriate the gas company, the electric power company and the streetcar company, was not a Marxist but an anti-Semitic Socialist: Karl Lueger, elected as Lord Mayor of Vienna in 1897. As Joseph Stalin showed, some fifty years later, Marxism and anti-Semitism can easily be combined. Of course, Stalin was no longer quite sane toward the end of his life. But it was not just paranoia that made Stalin embark in the late 1940s on an anti-Semitic campaign. A master politician, he surely realized the failure of Marxism as a creed and reached for the anti-Semitic alternative to rejuvenate a dying socialism and a paralyzed Communist Party.

From the beginning, that is, from the 1880s on, Marxist and anti-Semitic "national" socialism were thus in parallel and competing with each other for the succession to "bourgeois" liberalism. Before the 1873 crash, two young men, Victor Adler and Georg von Schönerer, had been the rising stars of Austrian liberalism, close allies and good friends. Within five years, they had become bitter enemies. Adler emerged as the continent's most respected Marxist leader and

Schönerer founded the first anti-Semitic political party. Adolf Hitler would put into practice in Germany sixty years later what he had imbibed from Schönerer while a young drifter in Vienna in the years before World War I.

Before 1873, Karl Marx was a fairly obscure "oddball," eking out a precarious living as a journalist. Five years later he had become a major intellectual figure with disciples throughout Europe and even in America. Within twenty years after 1873, Marxist Socialists had become the single largest party in every major continental European country, in France and Italy, Germany and Austria, and even—though officially suppressed—in czarist Russia.

Ten years after the Vienna crash—between 1883 and 1888—Bismarck, the German chancellor, invented national health insurance and compulsory old-age insurance. This launched the "welfare state," in which government provides the safety net of Social Security. At the same time Great Britain and Austria began to push back the power of employers through factory inspection, health and safety rules, and restrictions on the employment of children and women. Even in the United States, far removed from European political trends, the 1880s brought a shift away from the unrestricted market with the Granger laws, the Interstate Commerce Commission to regulate the railroads, the Anti-Trust laws, and the first state laws regulating and restricting the securities business. In the United States, too, in the late 1880s, the first distinctly "anti-business" political movement arose: populism, with its demands for government control of Wall Street, for government control of farm prices, and for government control of working hours and wages. And around 1900 under populist leadership Lincoln, the capital of Nebraska, became the second city—following Vienna in Austria by a few years—to "socialize" the local power company, the local gas company, and the local streetcar company.

By the mid-nineties anti-Semitism, too, had become a major political force. In 1894, Captain Alfred Dreyfus was convicted in France as a spy on trumped-up changes. The Dreyfus trial triggered an explosion of anti-Semitism of which the pro-Nazi Vichy government of World War II was the direct descendant. In 1895, the court preacher of the German emperor, Adolf Stöcker, founded a Socialist and anti-Semitic party in Berlin in an open bid to mobilize the country's "anti-capitalists." And, a year later, as already said, the Austrians selected the first anti-Semite to high political office as Lord Mayor of Vienna.

With the Dreyfus Affair, totalitarianism emerged fully fledged. Within two years after Dreyfus had been falsely accused of having been a spy in German pay, everyone in France knew that he was innocent. Indeed, by that time the identity of the real spy was an open secret. Yet the demand for Dreyfus's rehabilitation was met with "who cares whether Dreyfus is innocent, what matters is the good of the army." This is the essence of totalitarianism: the assertion that the collective, the party, the state, the Aryan race, is the absolute. The assertion that the good of the army was "truth," and the ultimate criterion, rallied French public opinion against Dreyfus. Ten years later, Dreyfus was rehabilitated. But by that time Lenin had already defined "truth" as whatever helps, strengthens, and advances the "Party"—the definition on which all later totalitarian regimes have been based: his own, Mussolini's, Hitler's, and Mao's.

For one hundred years, following the Vienna Stock Market crash of 1873, government control of the economy and government direction of society were the "progressive" causes. The great political debate was not over the welfare state. It was between believers in a "welfare state" in which there are democratic and legal restraints on government and on its control of economy and society, and the believers in totalitarianism either of the Marxist or of the anti-Semitic persuasion, who preached and practiced absolute, unrestricted government power.

The 1973 Divide

Economically, the "oil shock" of 1973 and President Nixon's decision, two years earlier, to let the dollar "float" can also be considered non-events. An economic statistician who looks only at figures such as gross national product, economic growth rates, foreign-trade statistics, and so on, would see little effect beyond immediate, short-term, and statistically insignificant fluctuations. Similarly, if one looks only at how institutions behave, the student rebellions of the late 1960s—the momentous, earthshaking, headline-making events in Japan, in France, in Germany, in Italy, in the United States—must also be considered non-events. They made no difference whatever in the way any one of these institutions— governments, universities, society altogether—behaves.

And yet the period of 1968–73 is a divide fully comparable to 1873. Where 1873 was the end of the Liberal era, 1973 marked the end of the era in which government was the "progressive" cause. It ended the era dominated by the doctrines and policies first formulated in the 1870s, those of Liberal Democrats or Social Democrats, of Marxist Socialists or National Socialists. All these doctrines are rapidly becoming as ineffectual as laissez-faire liberalism became after 1873.

Political slogans outlive political reality. They are the smile on the face of politics' Cheshire Cat. The political slogans of 1850, which expressed the political beliefs of the great Liberal generation of Prince Albert, Queen Victoria's prince consort, of John Stuart Mill, and of the 1848 revolutionaries on the European continent, are still common coinage among today's neoconservatives—albeit mostly small change. The slogans of the "welfare state" century will similarly be with us for a long time yet. But just as the Liberals had ceased to have much political relevance by 1900—even though they remained highly visible, highly vocal, and highly respectable for a long time—the political doctrines which the slogans of the welfare state or of communism reflect have ceased to have much relevance or reality, politically, socially, even economically. The slogans can still serve as brakes on action. They are unlikely any longer to provide guides to action or motive power.

The slogans of the New Deal may provide stirring political rhetoric in American elections for years to come. What they do not do, as several campaigns have shown by now, is attract enough votes to get elected, let alone guidance as to what to do when in power. They too are no more than the smile on the face of the Cheshire Cat—with nothing else left of the beast.

2

NO MORE SALVATION
BY SOCIETY

"As long as it does not threaten the Communist Party's monopoly of power, it's socialism." This is the new "Party line" preached by Mikhail Gorbachev in Russia and by Xiaoping Deng in China. But this is not a new pragmatism, as the Western press calls it. It is the ideology of naked power (and very old). It totally abjures everything that communism of any kind—or socialism for that matter—ever stood for. It is as if the Pope declared that as long as Catholics pay the Peter's Pence to Rome, it does not matter whether they believe in Christ or not.

This policy brazenly recants the fundamental claim that allowed Karl Marx to call his doctrine *scientific* socialism: the promise of an everlasting society that achieves both social perfection and individual perfection, a society that establishes the earthly paradise. It was this belief in salvation by society that gave Marxism its tremendous appeal. Yet no one except a small handful of superannuated party hacks was surprised by Gorbachev's ideology of power. Everybody else—and especially in the Communist countries—had much earlier lost all faith in salvation by society. Everybody else had become not a pragmatist but a cynic.

Mr. Gorbachev in Russia, and Mr. Deng and his successors in China, may succeed in maintaining their party's monopoly of power or even in reviving the economy. But one thing they cannot restore is the belief in salvation by society, whether through communism or any other ism. It is gone for good. The belief in salvation by society is equally gone in non-Communist countries. No one—except perhaps the "liberation theologians" in South America—believes any more in the power of social action to create a perfect society, or even to bring society closer to such an ideal, or in fundamentally changing the individual to produce the "new Adam."

Fifty years ago, such beliefs were commonplace. Not only Socialists but the great majority of political thinkers all over the world believed that social action—and especially the abolition of private property—would fundamentally change the human being. There would be Socialist Man, Nazi Man, Communist Man, and so on. The differences were not over the basic creed itself but over the speed of advance, over which particular action would be most productive. The main argument was over means. Should it be the role of politics and government to remove obstacles to social perfectibility—what today would be called "neoconservative" and sixty years ago was called "Liberal"? Or should government actively create new institutions and new conditions? *And now this is gone.*

Government will not "wither away"; there are few signs thereof. But anyone who now proclaims the "Great Society" as Lyndon Baines Johnson did only twenty years ago would be laughed out of court. We debate specific measures. We question whether government should subsidize this activity or prohibit that one. Each policy will be argued on its own cost/benefit ratio. Its chances for success will be debated: Is forbidding addictive drugs more likely to curb drug abuse than legalizing them? Is this or that measure likely to attract votes, keep a party in power, or drive out the "ins"?

Of course, there are still people—and probably will be for a good long time—who call themselves "Socialist" or "Labor." But what this now means is exemplified by François Mitterand, the president of France since 1981. When he came to power Mitterand was the last truly committed Social Democrat in Europe, heir to the programs, the hopes, the promises of the 1930s. Within one hundred eighty days, reality—in the form of a capital flight from France—forced him to reverse course. Mitterand's Socialist government became almost overnight the most nearly pro-capitalist government in the Western world. Since 1982 socialism in Mitterand's France has meant putting in as chief executives of nationalized industries friends and supporters of the ruling party. Socialism in France now is whatever improves the Socialist Party's hold on power. Contrast this with what happened fifty years earlier, in 1931, during Great Britain's desperate economic crisis, when a Socialist prime minister, Ramsay MacDonald, put short-range economic needs ahead of Socialist principles. Mac-Donald was soundly derided as a traitor and immediately lost all respect. Mitterand became a hero.

John F. Kennedy was the first American President in this century who did not even pretend to have a "program" except the conquest of power. He remains to this day a hero and a cult figure even though he accomplished little in his three years as President. And Lyndon B. Johnson, the last American President perhaps who still believed in salvation by society, became the butt of ridicule for his Great Society. His War on Poverty has become a byword for failure. Salvation by society failed the most where it promised the most, in the Communist countries. But it also failed in the West. Practically no government program enacted since the 1950s in the Western world—or in the Communist countries—has been successful. The last one to make a real difference perhaps was the British National Health Service, enacted in 1946–47. It is still hugely popular in the United Kingdom, but it is in serious and deepening crisis.

Equally important, we have increasingly come to doubt that there is "one right answer" to any social problem. There are wrong answers, to be sure. But we now know that social situations, social behavior, social problems are much too complex to admit a simple "right answer." If they can be solved at all, they always have several solutions—and none is quite right. We now know that there is no one right way to teach or to learn. There is a right way for one student and a different right way for another student. There is no one right way to protect the environment against industrial waste and pollutants. In some situations prohibitions and bans are appropriate, in others fines. In still others non-pollution needs to be made profitable. To have popular appeal, any promise of "Salvation by Society" must however be able to say, "This is the only way," or at least, "This is the best way by far." We thus find ourselves at the end of two centuries of Western history.

The belief in salvation by faith dominated medieval Europe. Revived in the Protestant Reformation of the sixteenth century, it had waned by the middle of the seventeenth century. To be sure, each religious denomination proclaimed—and still proclaims—its way as "the only right way." But by the middle of the seventeenth century it had become widely accepted that faith was a personal matter. This did not mean that religious persecutions stopped; there were still some even in the nineteenth-century West. And not until the middle of the nineteenth century did political disabilities based on religion totally disappear even in Western countries. But the belief that religious faith could create the City of God on earth had disappeared—or become irrelevant—a hundred years earlier.

The void created by the disappearance of the belief in salvation through faith was filled in the mid-1700s by the emergence of the belief in salvation by society, that is, by a temporal social order, embodied in an equally temporal government. This belief was first enunciated by Jean-Jacques Rousseau in France. Thirty years later, Jeremy Bentham in England worked it up into a political system. It was cast in its permanent form, into a "scientific" absolutism, by the "father of sociology," Auguste Comte, and by G. W. F. Hegel in Germany. Those two then "begat" Marx. Lenin, Hitler, and Mao were all Marx's children. In the rise of the West to world dominance, superiority in machines, money, and guns was probably less important than the promise of salvation by society. *And now it is gone.*

The end of the belief in salvation by society spells the death of the most pervasive delusion of the last two hundred years: the mystique of The Revolution. It was buried when Mikhail Gorbachev dared call Lenin's October Revolution a "historical event"—it had always, in the Communist lexicon, been "the end of time." To be sure, revolutions will continue to occur as they have occurred in the past: coups d'état, power grabs, rebellions against tyrannical governments, and, above all, "collapses from within" which, throughout history, have been the most frequent cause of violent overthrow of government. A few of these revolutions will improve matters; others will simply replace King Log by King Stork. But The Revolution was something quite different. It was a messianic event, a secular second coming, which would restore to pristine purity both human society and human being. To be sure, The Revolution would be violent. But after the "oppressed proletariat" had thrown off its shackles—or the virtuous Aryans had driven out the Jews—the new dawn would usher in Utopia. The defeated "radicals" of the French Revolution were the first to have this messianic vision in 1794 as their ideal society collapsed around them into the Terror and then into the Counterrevolution of the Directoire. The vision was revived after the failure of the 1848 revolutions in continental Europe. It became central to Marx and Marxism when the Paris Commune of 1871 ended in bloody massacre and military suppression. It still sustained Mao's followers in the "Great Cultural Revolution" in China only fifteen years ago. But even the terrorists who kill and burn in the name of The Revolution—the small band of Maoists, for instance, who terrorize the Peruvian Andes—no longer believe in the messianic promise. They destroy not because they hope but because they despair.

There may well be new messianic movements. The disappearance of the belief in salvation by society and in the second coming of a secular revolution may call forth new prophets and new messiahs. But these new messianic movements are likely to be anti-society and based on the assertion that there can be salvation only outside society, only in and through the person, perhaps even only in and through withdrawal from society.

The Reagan Revolution in the United States and the Thatcher Revolution in Great Britain (or Mr. Gorbachev's *Perestroika* in the Soviet Union) are not "anti-government," for all their rhetoric. Both President Reagan and Prime Minister Thatcher have consistently increased the size and scope of their respective governments—and Chairman Gorbachev may well do likewise. The importance of these developments—and of Mr. Deng's "New China"—is that they abandon salvation by society. They do not look upon government as the organ to produce a better, let alone a perfect, society. They see the function of government in specifics: to improve American competitiveness; to cut back the power of the British trade unions; to make homeowners out of renters in British council housing; to improve productivity on the Russian farm; to reduce the corruption in Chinese government and Communist Party; and so on. We are seeing in politics what happened when "modern" medicine first began around 1700: a turning away from panaceas to specific diagnosis and the search for specific remedies against specific ills. This new focus did not mean less medicine and fewer doctors; it has meant far more medicine and many more doctors. Similarly, the change in politics need not mean less government and fewer government measures. But it does mean that the role and function of government is perceived as different—and so is its ultimate aim.

The death of the belief in salvation by society, which for two hundred years had been the most dynamic force in the politics of the West and increasingly in politics worldwide, creates a void. The emergence of fundamentalist Islam is an attempt to fill this void. It is the result of disenchantment alike with the welfare state of the "democratic" West and with Communist Utopia. The strong resurgence of religion as an element in public life in the United States, the resurgence of evangelical and pastoral churches, is in some measure a reaction against the disappearance of the secular faith in salvation by society. The 1988 election campaign in the United States proved decisively, however, that we are not going to return to a belief in salvation by faith as major political factor, despite all the publicity given to the "Moral Majority." Nor is a return to early nineteenth-century laissez-faire very likely either. For laissez-faire too promised salvation by society: to remove all obstacles to the pursuit of individual gain would in the end produce a perfect—or at least the best possible—society.

The last Western politician of first rank to believe in salvation by society was Willy Brandt, the German Socialist chancellor of the early 1970s. His successor as leader of the German Socialists, Helmut Schmidt, was a "stoic" rather than a "believer." He had only one political ideology, namely, decency. Otherwise he believed in—and successfully practiced—pragmatic politics, which dealt with short-term, ad hoc problems rather than with issues. His guiding principles were not principles at all. They were effectiveness, efficiency, and the ratio between costs and benefits. His successor, the Christian Democrat Helmut Kohl, equally has no "principles" other than not to have any. What matters to Kohl is whether things work or do not work. The touchstone for politics increasingly is what is likely to keep a party in power or help it get into power.

Is this enough to provide the integration of factions, of interest groups, of the diversity of short-term pressures that characterize a modern complex society? Is it enough to provide governance, leadership, policy?

3

THE END OF FDR'S AMERICA

Salvation by society was the most visible organizing political principle. It was not, however, the only one. Since the 1890s it has had a competitor which gained dominance first in the United States and then in post-World War II Japan. This principle is the integration of the body politic through major "interest blocs"—into what might be called the "economic estates of the realm," to use an old term of political theory. It opposes economic promise to the Utopia of salvation by society.

This concept goes back all the way to the Roman Republic. It became political reality only at the end of the nineteenth century, and in the United States. By that time Bismarck's welfare state was beginning to triumph over class war—the purpose for which Bismarck had expressly designed it. Marxist Socialists in Western and Central Europe were rapidly changing into "revisionist" Social Democrats and becoming bourgeois. In the United States, though, a new and vocal populism was emerging that was in many ways more "anti" and more "radical" than the European left. To counter this threat of divisive class war—the occasion was the 1896 presidential election—an American politician, Mark Hanna, invented a new political integration in which major economic interests (the economic estates of the realm) are held together by their common interest in what we would now call economic development; then it was called prosperity.

Mark Hanna was one of the true innovators in the history of politics. Very few American politicians are his equals, excepting only the authors of the *Federalist Papers.* Yet he has had a bad press. The reason for this is his success: he deflected American politics away from ideology, and for this the political scientists have never forgiven him. It is axiomatic for them that respectable politics is ideological politics. Respectable politics must deal with issues rather than with performance. But whatever has worked in American politics for almost a century has been based on Mark Hanna's economic interests and their political integration. They immediately gave victory and power to Hanna's Republican Party. And when the Republican Party split of 1912 gave back victory to the Democrats, their winning candidate, Woodrow Wilson, was as convinced an anti-ideological, interest-group politician as Hanna had ever been. Mark Hanna laid the intellectual foundations and created to a large extent the organization needed to convert his political concepts into political performance. He did not found the Republican Party; but he recreated it.

Forty years later, a Democrat, Franklin D. Roosevelt, completed Mark Hanna's edifice. Roosevelt, as everybody knows, did not win in 1932; Herbert Hoover lost. But Roosevelt had been nominated in 1932 over the party's long-time favorite, Al Smith, precisely because he repudiated Smith's attempt to remake American politics in Europe's ideological image. As soon as he had moved into the White House, Roosevelt started to rebuild Hanna's economic integration which the Great Depression had shattered. He added to it a role for government as a dynamic, life-giving, innovative force. Government would not only be the channel through which Hanna's interest blocs—farmer, labor, business—would merge into common action. It would balance the three. It would make sure that no one group would be oppressed and exploited by any of the others, but also that no one group would dominate the others. Roosevelt's government was to be both integrator and balance wheel. It was to use its power to maintain social equilibrium.

Politically and socially FDR's administration may have been the most successful the United States has ever seen, despite the fact that every one of his economic policies misfired. The traditional businessman saw FDR as a "radical," putting labor into the saddle. But FDR made sure that the labor unions did not, as they had in Europe, become a separate political force, controlling either the legislature or the administration. And while much of FDR's rhetoric was antibusiness, his actions, from the beginning, aimed at creating the purchasing power to generate consumer demand and with it profits for business. Similarly, FDR greatly increased support for the farmer. But while under his predecessor farm policy had been protectionist, FDR's farm policy was aimed— in conscious continuity from Mark Hanna—at making American farming increasingly more productive. And by adding "reform" to "recovery," that is, by adding the promise of social justice to Mark Hanna's prosperity, Roosevelt created hope.

Economically, the United States did not even begin to recover until it moved into a war economy in 1940 and 1941. Socially and politically, however, the United States, alone of all the major Western countries, had fully recovered, had indeed regained momentum, within a year or eighteen months after Roosevelt took over. Despite the closing of the banks, catastrophic unemployment, and droughts and dust storms that ravaged farm economy and farm society, the

American people had come to see themselves by 1935 as victorious and as leaders.

No government anywhere in this century has proven more successful. No other government in this century of ideological cleavages and civil wars has been able to create greater national cohesion. This explains why FDR's America in the thirties became the guiding light and inspiration all over the globe—to the point where it became "the enemy" for the true radicals. This by the way is also the most plausible explanation for what is otherwise inexplicable: Hitler's completely unnecessary declaration of war against the United States after the Japanese attacked Pearl Harbor (which in the last analysis doomed Nazi Germany). It also explains why, immediately after World War II, the Soviet Union had to make the United States its real "enemy" even though the U.S. government and the American people were more than willing to support their wartime ally, to subsidize it, and to be friends with it. FDR's tradition continued through the administration of Harry Truman. Truman was perhaps even more conscious than FDR himself of the concepts underlying FDR's New Deal. The FDR tradition reached its apogee under Dwight Eisenhower, who knew it to be his historical mission to codify the New Deal but also to recapture for the Republican Party the integrating power of Mark Hanna's vision.

Political integration through the economic promise of prosperity—as against political ideology—is generally considered to work "only in America." But that is simply not true. It has done as well in totally alien soil as it ever did in Mark Hanna's or FDR's native country. The Japanese government since World War II—the most effective government of the last thirty-five years—has been based on Mark Hanna's integration by economic interests. There is, of course, nothing in the American political system that remotely resembles the unique position and power of the Japanese Civil Service. Nor is there anything in the Japanese system that remotely resembles the position and power of America's unique political institution, the non-politician and non-bureaucrat "insiders" and Washington "veterans"—lawyers, journalists, professors, business executives—who, several thousand strong, return again and again to government service under Republicans and Democrats alike, and who hold practically all decision-making jobs in both the major departments of government, and on the staffs of the major congressional committees. There are also some features of the Liberal Democratic Party that has been in power in Japan since 1950 which are uniquely Japanese (though not nearly as many as most Japanese and Westerners alike assume). But the Japanese party's concepts and its structure are pretty much those of Roosevelt's Democratic Party of the 1930s and even more those of Coolidge's Republican Party of the 1920s: the same factions, the same political bosses dominating a major city or region, the same continuously shifting coalitions between major interest groups; and also the same "deals" and the same political corruption of local and regional party machines.

The American example also enabled Western Europe in large part to recover politically and socially as well as economically. The old parties with their ideological labels remained. But only the Communists in southern Europe actually remained "ideological" and dedicated to "salvation by society," which is why they have almost ceased to matter. Konrad Adenauer and Helmut Schmidt in Germany; Charles de Gaulle and François Mitterand in France; Margaret Thatcher in Britain; Alcide de Gaspari and Bettino Craxi in Italy, all achieved their political successes through anti-ideological, interest-bloc integration. None of them paid the slightest attention to the ideological manifestos of their own parties.

But by now Mark Hanna's and Franklin D. Roosevelt's integration through economic interests is as dated as is integration through salvation by society. The last American President to try it was Lyndon Johnson. His Great Society simply did not work as political integration as it would have worked twenty years earlier. Every attempt since to rekindle Hanna and Roosevelt's vision has been a disaster. Rarely in American history has there been a more competent, more decent, more experienced presidential candidate in American history than Walter Mondale in 1984—and few who lost more thoroughly. His attempt to re-forge the interest-group coalition of FDR's America made him sound hopelessly obsolete; few people under age fifty could even figure out what he was talking about. Four years later, in 1988, Michael Dukakis tried to find and mobilize new "interest blocs," especially the "middle class"—without alienating the old ones. It did not work either.

Outside of the United States, interest-bloc integration is also proving less and less capable of providing political integration. The Liberal Democrats still win every Japanese election, but only because the opposition parties are all ideological believers in salvation by society, which makes them even less attractive. One reason why interest-bloc integration no longer works is that the economic "interest groups" are disappearing as distinct entities and self-conscious identities. Neither "farmer" nor "labor" has the numerical strength or the political importance to be an "economic estate" any more in any developed country. In Mark Hanna's America, farmers were half the population. When Franklin D. Roosevelt started, labor was close to two fifths of the population. Now farmers are no more than 3 percent of the population, and traditional "blue-collar" labor is at best one fifth. "Business" as an economic estate of the realm also no longer exists. The "business interest" that Mark Hanna mobilized for political power was not General Motors or Citibank. It was the shoe repairman, the tavern owner, the cabinetmaker in the small town. There are still plenty of them around. But they do not see themselves as "business" or as a separate interest group.

Secondly, and more important, none of these groups is socially distinct any more. What gave each its political unity and political identification was actually not a common economic interest. Livestock breeders are "farmers," but all along they have had very different economic interests from dairy farmers or tobacco growers. Skilled craftsmen have very different economic interests from the unskilled mass-production worker who became the majority of "American labor" during the 1920s. What made these groups distinct and capable of united action was what we today call culture. They were far more identified socially then they were identified economically. There was the "self-respecting workingman" and there was "rural society." And then there were "businessmen," in both small towns and big cities. Each of these groups read different newspapers, largely went to different churches, and usually lived in different parts of town. Each had distinct values and a distinct lifestyle. Above all, each group had a clear and distinct view of itself. They were not "class-conscious" in Marxist terms. Nor did they necessarily believe that they were exploited by the other groups and classes in society—at least not after Mark Hanna's vision of their common interest in prosperity. Each was extremely conscious, however, that it was leading a different life, played a different role, and occupied a different place in society.

Both Mark Hanna and Franklin D. Roosevelt used "economic interest" as code words. What they meant—and both men probably knew it—was social and cultural values and styles. They talked quantities; they meant qualities. There is little left today of these values and styles. The remainders, such as the "cloth cap" worker of Northern England and Scotland, are now considered "backward." So are the farmers of Sicily. The American livestock breeder or the raiser of broiler chickens in an automated henhouse still thinks of himself as a farmer; but he has probably the greatest degree of computer literacy of any occupational group in the world. The blue-collar automobile workers in Detroit are clearly workers; but in their lifestyle there is little left of the working class except a preference for beer over wine. Otherwise, as the union representative in one of America's most militant automobile plants reminded me not so long ago, the union members' concerns are their motor homes, the fishing cabin in the North Woods, and their retirement pensions. They see exactly the same television programs as everybody else in American society. They buy the same consumer goods in the same supermarkets. They take the same vacations. They do different work, but they no longer lead different lives. They define their status not through their economic interests but through their *spending power*.

Thirdly, the new majority, the "knowledge worker," does not fit any interest-group definition. Knowledge workers are neither farmers nor labor nor business; they are employees of organizations. Yet they are not "proletarians" and do not feel "exploited" as a class. Collectively, they are the only "capitalists" through their pension funds. Many of them are themselves bosses and have "subordinates." Yet they also have a boss themselves. They are not middle class, either. They are, to coin a term, "uniclass"—though some of them make more money than others. It makes absolutely no difference to their economic or social position whether they work for a business, a hospital, or a university. Knowledge workers who move from accounting work in a business to accounting work in a hospital are not changing social or economic position. They are changing a job.

The great bulk of people in modern developed societies are employees of organizations. And the more education they have, the more likely they are to spend all their working life as employees of organizations. Yet this status implies no specific economic or social interest, no specific economic or social culture, and very little by way of issues. They simply defy the concept of society on which Mark Hanna's and Franklin D. Roosevelt's America were based. But so far there is no political concept, no political integration that fits them.

4

WHEN THE RUSSIAN EMPIRE
IS GONE

Two of the most significant events in modern history took place a few years before the 1873 "divide": the Indian Mutiny of 1857 and the Meiji Restoration in Japan ten years later, in 1867. The first ensured the "westernization" of the globe; the second its "decolonization."

The great Swiss historian Jakob Burckhardt was one of the very few contemporaries who immediately understood that the 1870s were a major turning point, and he said so in the prophetic lectures he gave in the early 1870s. Today the lectures, entitled *Weltgeschichtliche Betrachtungen* or *Reflections on World History* (the English translation was published in 1943 under the title *Force and Freedom*) are considered a classic. But despite his great reputation as a historian, nobody believed Burckhardt. His book was not even published until 1906, nine years after his death. Burckhardt knew and loved Oriental art and literature. But he dismissed both the Indian Mutiny and the Meiji Restoration as irrelevant. To him, and to his contemporaries, Western history was "world history." With the

Indian Mutiny and the Meiji Restoration, however, world history ceased to be "Western" history.

The Indian Mutiny was a desperate attempt to stop westernization. It failed when the victorious mutineers realized that they had no one and nothing to put in place of their almost-ousted British masters. Their collapse ensured the world dominance of Western technology, Western social organization, Western industrial economy, Western science, Western education. Attempts to get rid of the West continued, culminating in the Boxer Rebellion in China in 1900, forty-three years after the Indian Mutiny. More recently, the Ayatollah Khomeini's revolution in Iran in the 1980s was still another attempt to get rid of the West. But since the Indian Mutiny, all such attempts have been foredoomed to failure. Even the Ayatollah could fight the West only by using money paid by the West for Iranian oil to buy Western technology and Western arms.

The meaning of the Indian Mutiny and its failure was read clearly by Europeans of the time. It triggered the colonial race which began after 1860 and which, within forty years, had brought most of the non-Western world in Asia and Africa under the political control of Western powers—Great Britain, France, Belgium, Germany, and in the end even the United States. The Indian Mutiny convinced the Western powers that the entire globe would become westernized. This then led them to the conclusion that they should and could take political, military, and economic control of the entire world, and make it into an extension of Western culture and of Western empires.

Japan hesitated for fifteen years after Commodore Perry's "Black ships" first anchored off Yokohama in 1853. But then, in 1867, it decided to become thoroughly "Western" but to retain control of both the process of westernization and the ensuing government, society, economy, and technology. This decision was dismissed by practically all Western contemporaries—as it was by Burckhardt—as insignificant and indeed trivial, next to the triumphant onrush of Western power throughout the rest of the globe. Yet, in the end, Japan prevailed. The Japanese approach—to be modern, that is, westernized, but under native, non-Western control—in the end defeated the West. By embracing the West, Japan escaped its domination. Japan lost World War II in one of the most decisive military defeats in history. Japan also did not attain its own political ends, to become a dominant colonial power. Still, politically, it was the West that was defeated. Japan succeeded in pushing the West out of Asia and in discrediting the Western colonial powers. This forced the West to relinquish control of the westernized but non-Western world—in Asia but soon also in Africa.

Everywhere, since World War II, the non-Western world has refashioned itself after the model the Japanese first established in the Meiji Restoration in 1867. It has become westernized but under native control. This is what "anti-colonialism" basically means. It does not mean a return to pre-colonial status. Even Iran under the Ayatollah is not trying to restore eighteenth-century Persia but to develop a modern Iran, with the technology, the industry, the military, the engineering, of the West but the religion and values of early Islam. This is not so different from Japan's attempt in the 1870s to combine an English-type parliament with a return to the God-Emperor of the Nara and Heian periods a thousand years earlier.

In all the non-Western countries—whether they are fundamentalist, like the Ayatollah's Iran and Saudi Arabia, or secular; whether they repudiate their own past as did Mao's China or try to revive it as some of the African countries do—the basic structure is built out of concepts and institutions imported from the West. And so are the dominant ideas. These countries call themselves Democratic, Socialist, Communist. They speak of the welfare state. They all have large armies organized on Western models and equipped with the latest Western arms; they all have a central bank; they all attempt economic development. They send students for their education to the West. At the same time they are determined to maintain in their own hands control of these Western concepts, and Western institutions, and to exercise control through their own local and native power structure as Japan did after the Meiji Restoration.

The Last Colonial Power

But there is still one large colonial power left, one large area where history is still "European" history, and power and government are still exercised by Europeans only: the Russian Empire. Within twenty-five years, if not sooner, the Russian Empire too will have disappeared—or at least it will have changed from European into post-European and primarily Asian. Everything needed to bring this about has already happened. The only question is how fast the process will be and whether it will lead to a dismemberment of the empire or to its restructuring. This process will occur whether the reform movement begun in 1982 by Mikhail Gorbachev succeeds or not. In fact, the more Gorbachev's *Perestroika* succeeds in reviving a decaying Russian economy, the faster will the Russian Empire unravel.

Perestroika is a "revolution from above"—and they rarely succeed. Indeed, *Perestroika* bears a striking resemblance to Europe's last revolution from above, the utterly unsuccessful attempt of another "enlightened despot," the eighteenth-century Emperor Joseph II, to turn around and revive his stagnant, decaying Austrian Empire. Still there have been two "revolutions from above" that had lasting results, and both were Russian. One created the Russia we now know, the revolution from above of Ivan the Terrible. The second was the forced westernization of Peter the Great. One cannot therefore be sure that Mr. Gorbachev's attempt will have no results. But the Soviet economy, however serious its decay, is Mr. Gorbachev's minor problem. The central problem is the threat of the empire's disintegration under the pressures of nationalism and anti-colonialism.

The Russian Empire differs from the colonial empires of the Western powers in being land-based. But like them it rests on the subordination of other nationalities—Ukrainians, Estonians, Letts, Latvians, Caucasians in its European West, a dozen Mongolian, Turkish, and Tartar people in its Asian East. The nationalities problem is by no means new to Russia. A deliberate policy of Russianization made it increasingly acute under the czar. With very few exceptions (such as the old German-speaking universities in the Baltic countries) higher education was entirely in Russian, whatever the native tongue of the student. Russian was the official language and the only one allowed in business or the military. Resentment against Russianization was a major factor in the Bolsheviks' victory. Lenin's promise to give all nationalities full cultural and educational autonomy obtained for him the support of the Lett Sharpshooters, one of the czar's crack regiments. Without them the October Revolution could not have succeeded.

By the late 1920s it was becoming clear that Lenin's nationalities policy would not work. In fact, Stalin's first purge victims in the thirties were the educational leaders who ten years earlier fashioned Lenin's policy. By 1927 or 1928 they began to urge Stalin, himself a Georgian, to revise Lenin's policy. They pointed out that non-Russians, and especially Asians, were rapidly becoming literate in their own tongues but unlike their predecessors under the czar, they were not forced to learn Russian. This would create a new nationalities problem—and for their warning Stalin had them shot. Sixty years later their prophecy has come true. But this time it is not only the non-Russians in Europe who are the problem. The Asians may be more difficult still.

* * *

By the year 2000 half the population of the Soviet Union will consist of non-Europeans, and close to half of this non-European, Asian population, will be Moslems. For the last forty years, since the end of World War II, European Russia has had the demographics of a developed European country, with very low birth rates—to the point where European Russia has suffered actual population shrinkage. Asian Russia, by contrast, has had the demographics of a developing country, that is, a rapid fall in infant mortality with continuing high birth rates. The non-European population of Asian Russia may now have the fastest growth rates in the world, exceeding even those of Latin America.

As the European population of Russia ages and actually shrinks, the Soviet Union will increasingly have to rely upon non-Europeans. There is already a labor shortage on the land, with a rapidly aging rural population—and, what is worse, with competent people fleeing the land. In industry, the Russians will either have to bring Asian workers into the European heartland, which is bound to be fiercely resisted by highly xenophobic Russians, or they will have to move production to where the labor is, into Asia, and thus risk losing control. Probably most serious is the dilemma of the armed forces. To maintain its military strength, the Soviet Union will increasingly have to draw upon Asians. But historically Asians have never fought under Russian command—as was again proven in Afghanistan. Russia will either have to cut its military forces drastically or risk losing control over them to increasingly anti-Russian Asians. Clearly it was these demographic considerations that made Mr. Gorbachev decide in the fall of 1988 unilaterally to reduce the strength of the Soviet Army by 500,000 men. His alternative—and a totally unacceptable one—would have been to entrust military control of Russia's European satellites to Asians.

The Asians in the Soviet Union are all literate now, but only a third of them are literate in Russian. Russia has however remained the language of government, the language of business, the language of science, as it was under the czar. There are practically no non-Europeans in command positions in the Russian military. There are practically no non-Europeans in command positions in the Russian economy. There are practically no non-Europeans in the Soviet Academy of Sciences. And there are never more than one or two non-Europeans in top party jobs, whether in the Politburo or the Central Committee.

This situation, predictably, will not last. Maybe the process of disintegration can be slowed. But once begun, it cannot be reversed. And it has begun. As we now know, it began well before Mr. Gorbachev took over; in the west, in the Baltic provinces and in the Ukraine; in the southeast, in the Crimea and the Caucausus; and in Central Asia. By now, in the late 1980s, Mr. Gorbachev has already been put on the defensive and forced to do what every colonial regime tries to do— always unsuccessfully. He has offered concessions to the people in the Baltic areas, but has threatened severe punishment to the Armenians and Azerbeijani in the southeast, and to Moslem Mongolians in Central Asia. Mikhail Gorbachev's *Perestroika* is thus an attempt to forge a new bond of unity through economic growth and development. Can it work? The answer is an almost certain no. If *Perestroika* fails, Russia will return to Stalinist repression. But if *Perestroika* works in the economy, it will also not have the desired unifying effect. Demographics alone will ensure its inability to defeat a rising anti-Russian nationalism. In fact, it will fast create ever more powerful centrifugal forces.

It is no accident that the most nationalist part of the Soviet Empire is its most prosperous part, the Baltic republics. The history of the Austria-Hungarian Empire shows why—and Austria-Hungary was similar to the Soviet Empire in being contiguous, all on land, and officially "non-national." The nationalities problem first arose in Austria in 1848 when the Hungarians revolted against Austrian rule. By 1867, the Hungarians had gained political, linguistic, and cultural autonomy. Austria also paid heavy and steadily increasing economic blackmail to Hungary's greedy large landowners to prevent their secession. But the other nationalities immediately demanded similar treatment, the Czechs first, then the Italians, the Croats, the Slovenes, the Poles. To counter their pressure, the liberals in Austria—like Mr. Gorbachev, the enlightened ones—discovered economic development as a supranational bond of unity. Economically, the policy worked like a charm. There are few parallels in history to the industrial growth of Bohemia, the Czech heartland, after 1870. By 1914 it had become one of the most industrialized and prosperous areas of Europe, with standards of living and productivity equal to Germany and ahead of France. Slovenia in the south and Croatia in the southeast of the Austrian Empire equally saw rapid economic growth. And so, though after a slow start, did the region around Cracow—it is still the industrial center of Poland.

Though economically a huge success, development was a political disaster in Austria. Instead of appeasing the nationalities, affluence only made them increasingly more nationalistic. The better off they became, the more fervently did the Czechs demand independence. The same thing happened in Slovenia, in Croatia, in Austrian Poland, and in Trieste— the Italian-speaking port which, by 1913, was among the wealthiest cities of Europe and the most stridently anti-Austrian. Yet Austria conceded to its nationalities infinitely more than Russia has ever been willing to give. All universities in the Soviet Empire are Russian universities whereas half the universities in the Austrian Empire were non-German: Hungarian, Czech, Slovenian, Croatian, Polish, and Ukrainian. The Austrian parliament accepted any number of languages.

Soldiers in the Austrian Army had to learn only a few command words in German; otherwise they used their own national languages. These concessions only created more pressure for increasing autonomy and ultimately for total independence. For nationalism and anti-colonialism are not the isms of peasants and proletarians; they are the isms of the bourgeoisie, and especially of the educated middle class of merchants, plant managers, and professionals. These groups are, of course, the first beneficiaries of economic growth.

What happened in British India teaches the same lesson. The British decided in the 1870s—at about the same time as the Austrians—to promote economic development so as to offer Indians, and especially educated Indians, tangible benefits of British rule. They pushed the construction of railroads and ports, created rural cooperatives and engineering schools, and promoted Indian export crops. Above all, they founded the Indian Congress to bring Britishers and educated Indians together in joint work on economic and social development. The economic and social results were substantial; modern India was largely created by these efforts. Politically, though, these efforts spawned the Indian Independence movement which, in 1947, accomplished what the Indian Mutiny, ninety years earlier, had failed to do: get rid of the British. Practically every single leader of the Independence movement came out of the Indian Congress.

What did not work in Austria and India is unlikely to work in Russia. As people become "westernized," more affluent, more mobile, more educated, they increasingly become more nationalist. They increasingly resent being "colonials," even if the yoke is a light one. They demand the "Japanese solution": to be westernized but under their own control, management, and government. There is thus no reason to believe that *Perestroika* can save the Russian Empire.

Three outcomes are possible. One is that Russia will split into two halves. Both the European half and the Asian half may then splinter even further into national groups—autonomous if not independent Baltic states; an autonomous if not independent Ukraine; autonomous if not independent Caucasian republics—with the same process taking place on the Asian side of the Urals. The European successors to the Russian Empire will then surely have to try to become part of Europe and may well have to accept political and, above all, economic subordination to Europe. Some Far Eastern successors may move closer to China. But where would the largest chunk go—the Central Asians, who are predominantly Moslems? The second possibility is Asian domination. But this surely means constant resistance of the European minority against the Asian majority. Finally, there is the possibility of some sort of confederation, loosely held together and in constant turmoil, as nationalities in and through their autonomous republics struggle with one another for power, each trying to dominate the rest.

Whatever the outcome, it will be neither "Russian" nor "Empire." The disintegration of the Russian Empire will create totally new realities in international politics—realities for which no one is as yet prepared, least of all the United States.

The period will be a turbulent and indeed a dangerous one. Russia will have to change fundamentally its relations with Europe. One cannot rule out the possibility that Russia under increasing internal pressure will try a military adventure and attempt an invasion of Western Europe. That a victorious war can "rejuvenate" is, after all, the most common delusion of political senility. The Austrians were overwhelmed by it in 1914, as were the Argentine generals when they seized the Falkland Islands in 1982. So was Napoleon, who decided to attack Russia in 1812 when he had been proven no longer invincible, first by the Austrian victories in 1809, and then, in Spain, by the victories of the Duke of Wellington. If the nationalist unrest in Russia spreads to its satellites in Europe and causes serious trouble in Hungary,

Poland, Czechoslovakia, or East Germany, a military excursion into Western Europe might well tempt the generals of Russia as much as such an "excursion" tempted the generals of Austria in 1914. There is need, in other words, to maintain both the political unity of the West and its military preparedness.

But there is also need to be ready for a total change in Russia's relationship with Western Europe. This would surely require major changes in Russia's political, economic, and social structure, and in its policies. It would almost certainly mean the end of NATO and of the American-European Alliance altogether. It would require a change in the government and policies of Russia's satellites in Europe—and almost certainly their rejection of both communism and Russian control. It might require military neutralization of Central Europe—from the Russian border to the Rhine. Yet it might be the only way in which European Russia could escape being dominated by Asian Russia. Any government in European Russia will be forced by its people to put freedom from Asian control very high on its priority list. The disintegration of the Russian Empire is likely to be far more traumatic for the mother country, European Russia, than the dissolution of their overseas empires was for Spain, Britain, France, the Netherlands, or Portugal earlier in this century. And the impact of the disintegration of the Russian Empire on Asia is going to be even greater. It will profoundly change the relations of both China and Japan to the rest of Asia, to each other, and to the West—especially the United States.

What It Means for the United States

For the United States, the disintegration of the Russian Empire means a total change in foreign policy, and in the assumptions that have undergirded American foreign policy since Woodrow Wilson abandoned non-interventionism in 1917. To be sure, Russia—whether Communist or post-Com-

munist—will cease to be a "superpower." But so will the
United States. In fact, there will be no "superpowers." There
will be no such thing as a "center" in world politics. It will be
increasingly difficult for the United States to have a "foreign
policy" at all—and returning to isolationism would not help,
would in fact be impossible.

As long as there was a British Empire with the British Navy
controlling the Seven Seas—throughout the nineteenth century—American foreign policy was clear. It consisted of the
Monroe Doctrine, which tried to keep America out of world
politics altogether. America could be isolationist. This period
came to an end with the decline of Europe. Since World War
I, the first priority of American foreign policy has increasingly
been to restore Europe. When Japan attacked in 1941, the
United States decided to give priority to the war in Europe
rather than concentrate on the Pacific. When the Cold War
began in the 1940s, it was the recovery of Europe and the
NATO military alliance on which the United States based its
foreign policy. This European orientation was, however, possible only because the Asian heartland was still controlled and
governed by a *European* power, Russia. From the U.S. vantage
point, all that was needed in Asia were forward bases—in the
Philippines or Japan—that protected America's flanks. Otherwise, relations in Europe with a European power, i.e., a
Europe-centered Russia, took care of Asia. Or rather, America's policies and actions in Asia—whether the Korean War,
the Vietnam War, or President Nixon's rapprochement with
Communist China—were essentially parts of America's European strategy to contain and counterbalance a *European*-cen-
tered Russia.

This is unlikely to prove adequate, let alone successful,
when Russia will have ceased to be a European power controlling Asia. But what policy is needed then—and how the
United States could even have a policy at all when Europe can
no longer be given priority—is quite impossible to anticipate.

Of all the new political realities this may turn out to be the toughest one for the United States.

North America as a New U.S. Concern

American foreign policy will be even further confused by the rapid emergence of North America as a major U.S. concern. For its neighbors, Mexico in the south and Canada in the north, relations to the giant next door have all along been *the* foreign policy concern. The United States, however, has usually paid little attention to its neighbors. The rapid regionalization of the world economy is creating a new "North America," and with it new opportunities and new problems.

America's southern neighbor, Mexico, is undergoing a transformation that will change U.S. relations with the Latin world. For more than a hundred years, since Benito Juárez, Mexican policy has been dominated by one goal: independence, and especially economic independence, from the threatening colossus of the north, the *Yanqui* neighbor, so different from Mexico in religion, culture, values, history, tradition—repulsive and alluring alike—and much too close. Juárez tried to maintain Mexican independence by keeping the country Indian and rural. His successor, Porfirio Díaz, tried to bring in European money, European bankers, European manufactures, to counterbalance the feared *Yanqui*. The failure of this effort led to Díaz's overthrow in 1911, followed by twenty years of civil war. The aim then became industrial self-sufficiency. Mexico pushed for highly protected domestic industry, producing exclusively for the Mexican domestic market and owned, in large part, by the Mexican government. For a good many years, especially after World War II, this seemed to work. But the policy collapsed into total ruin in the early 1980s, in part because of the collapse of the price of oil, but in much larger part because protectionism made the government corrupt and government-owned industry inefficient and uncompetitive.

One way out—maybe the only one—is abandonment of Mexico's century-old policy of economic independence and acceptance of economic integration with the United States. Integration is already an accomplished fact to a large extent. Mexico's most efficient and best-paying industries—the *maquiladora* plants along the U.S. border and some plants in the interior owned by American giants such as Ford and IBM—produce mainly (or entirely) for the U.S. market. And there is talk of a U.S.-Mexico Common Market. From the American point of view, economic integration would certainly be preferable to continued very heavy immigration from Mexico—the only way today in which many Mexicans can get access to paying jobs. Economically, it would also benefit Mexico, although the transition period would be very rough on a good many overprotected Mexican companies, their workers and their owners. But culturally and politically such a shift would be so traumatic as to threaten Mexico's political cohesion and perhaps even its political unity.

Without it, however, can Mexico survive? It has not yet really become one country. The north is largely Spanish-speaking; it has the industry and most of whatever fertile land there is in a country where the climate tends to be either too dry to grow decent crops (in much of the north) or too wet (in much of the south). The south—beginning around Oaxaca—is still predominantly rural and Indian, with Spanish spoken primarily in the cities. A good deal of the south is tribal and run by local chiefs, not so differently from the *caziques* who governed when the Spaniards first arrived four hundred fifty years ago. It was then that the greatest of the Christian missionaries, Bartoloméo de las Casas, said that "The Indian has to become a citizen before he can be a Christian." The Indians of southern Mexico have yet to become citizens.

Mexico is much too close for its problems not to affect the United States. Yet any conceivable U.S. policy toward Mexico is certain to be as unpopular in the States as it will be in Mexico. How long will the United States for instance continue to accept large numbers of Mexicans—among them increasingly both the country's best educated people and its poorest and least skilled ones—who flee Mexican joblessness, hunger, and poverty? Can Mexico itself long afford politically and socially the massive flight northward of its citizens and the growing brain drain? Can the United States accept a left-wing anti-American regime in Mexico? Can Mexico accept U.S. interference in its domestic policies? And will the United States be able, let alone willing, to accept economic integration when Mexican wages are one tenth of American ones, and farm products grown on Mexican irrigated land south of the border cost one third of what it costs to grow them north of the border?

Relations with America's northern neighbor, Canada, will equally become increasingly important. Whether the 1988 Free Trade Treaty between Canada and the United States becomes fully effective is relatively unimportant. Economically the two countries are already integrated. In fact, the lopsided dominance of Canadian markets by U.S. manufacturers that had prevailed since the twenties has largely been corrected, with Canadian manufacturers, Canadian financiers, Canadian real-estate developers becoming increasingly active on the U.S. side of the border. But Canada now faces a decade, or longer, in which the old question: What does Canada mean? will finally have to be faced. Is it one nation with three cultures—an Anglo-Scots one in the center, a French one in Quebec, a distinctly Canadian-American one in the Prairie provinces of the West? So far the only way to define "Canada" has been by its not being "U.S." But the more the economies of the two countries meld into each other, the less adequate will a negative definition be to hold together a huge, heterogeneous, and sparsely settled country. And the less adequately also will the U.S. traditional stance of

41

benign—and often not so very benign—neglect serve either Canada or the United States.

But the major "new reality" in international affairs—and by no means for the United States alone—remains the coming dissolution of the Russian Empire. This will complete the shift from "European" history to "world" history that began with the Indian Mutiny and Japan's Meiji Restoration. Is any government, any politician, any political thinker prepared for it?

5

NOW THAT ARMS ARE COUNTERPRODUCTIVE

November 15, 1988, should have been celebrated as a major milestone for humanity. On that day forty-three years and three months had passed since the last hostilities between major powers, the fighting between Japan and the United States that stopped on August 15, 1945. This tied the longest previous period without fighting between major powers: the forty-three years and three months between the end of the Franco-Prussian War in 1871 and the outbreak of World War I on August 1, 1914 (this period of "non-war" was marred by the war between Russia and Japan in 1905, but Japan was not then considered a major power). And the 1945–88 period of non-war greatly exceeded the celebrated twenty-nine years of major powers peace between Waterloo in 1815 and the Crimean War that pitted England and France against Russia in 1854.

There were good reasons why no one paid attention to the new record. These were hardly years of peace. Major powers did not fight each other, but four of them fought bloody wars: France in Algiers and Vietnam; the United States in Korea and Vietnam; China in Vietnam; and Russia in Afghanistan. The Middle East was at war during most of the time—Israel fighting the Arabs, and Iraq and Iran fighting each other for seven years. India and Pakistan fought a short but violent war. There were also any number of persistent and ferocious civil wars in Northern Ireland, in Central and South America, and in most of Africa.

Above all, these years saw the longest, biggest, and most widely spread arms race in history. Armaments have been the growth industry of—the post-World War II period—not computers, not telecommunications, not biotechnology, not even finance. The feverish arms race during the twenty years before August 1914 engaged only four countries: Great Britain, France, Germany, and Russia. Neither Italy nor Austria took part in it, nor, of course, did the United States. But only one major country, Japan, and two of the middle powers, Mexico and Canada, have stayed out of the arms race of the last forty years. Otherwise, it has engulfed the entire world. Even faster has been the explosive growth of military technology and of the destructive power of arms. By now even small and poor countries—Peru, Libya, Iraq—possess more, and more destructive, firepower than most of the Great Powers had when World War II began. There has been only one small step toward restraining the arms buildup: the U.S.-Russian treaty of 1988 limiting middle-range nuclear missiles. Otherwise, the arms race continues unabated. Arms, once the servant of policy, have become the master.

And yet arms have proven themselves counterproductive. They have become a major drain on economic performance and economic development—a major cause of Russia's economic crisis, of America's falling behind economically, and of the failure of development, especially in Latin America. Socially the army no longer functions as "the school of the nation," as the nineteenth century called it. Wherever the military took power, whether in Africa or in Latin America, it soon began to teach the wrong things: terror, torture, corruption. Politically, military aid—used these last forty years as never before—has proven unreliable to the point of being treacherous. After all, arms are proving impotent militarily. The Korean War ended in a draw despite the overwhelming superiority of the United States in men and arms. In all other conflicts between a major power and a small opponent the major power lost: the French in Algiers and Vietnam, the Americans in Vietnam, the Chinese in Vietnam, the Russians in Afghanistan. After winning four wars, Israel is no closer to victory than it was in the beginning. In seven years of bloody fighting, neither Iran nor Iraq—both armed to the teeth with the most modern of weapons—could show any military gains. And despite massive military assistance by various outside powers, the civil wars in Africa keep going on and on and on, without military decision in sight.

For any one of these cases of military malperformance and incompetence, one hears specific explanations. The United States lost in Vietnam in the sixties because the media stabbed the Army in the back, or because the generals fought the wrong kind of war. No doubt, after Russia's defeat in Afghanistan in the eighties, similar alibis went the rounds in Moscow. But generic phenomena require generic explanations. And the only generic explanation is that arms have lost their military capacity. They can win battles but can no longer decide wars. In an age of nuclear, chemical, and bacterial weapons, they can no longer defend their countries. Indeed, war can no longer be considered, in the famous words of Karl von Clausewitz, "the continuation of policy by other means." It has become the defeat of policy.

This first became apparent during America's war in Vietnam. In the early months of the Kennedy administration, I joined an advisory board to the Secretary of Defense on procurement and personnel, on which I served for nine years, almost to the end of the Vietnam War. The members of the board—three distinguished business leaders, three former high-ranking military officers, three academics like myself—were hardly "anti-military." Yet by the time he left the board, each of us had reached the same conclusion: arms had become counterproductive, even militarily. And the same conclusion, it was clear to all of us, had been reached by the military officers with whom we worked. Yet the arms buildup worldwide has only speeded up since then.

Cutting arms, however beneficial, is not enough. What is required is something far more difficult than disarmament. It is a reaffirmation of the role and importance of defense in the world's political system, especially a reaffirmation of the governmental monopoly on arms of destruction, combined with a return to defense and arms as the tools rather than the masters of policy they have become in the last forty years. What is required is rethinking the entire role and function of defense, of armaments, and of the military in the modern world, and a repositioning of the military in the body politic.

Arms and the Economy

Arms and military forces were pure burden and drain on the civilian economy and society for untold centuries. They also contributed little, if anything, to scientific or technological advance. The knight in shining armor may have been a glamorous figure, but he only took from society and gave nothing back to it. To keep one knight required four horses and at least six men; and to keep these in turn required the output of eight to ten farms. Yet the knight was not in the least concerned with defending the peasants to whom he owed his living. They only paid the costs. There was also no technology transfer from military to civilian production. Gunpowder came into use in the West in the fourteenth century. Not until five hundred years later, in the middle of the nineteenth century, were explosives first applied to mining, to tunneling, to road building, and to excavating harbors. Making the armor of the medieval knight required highly skilled armorers who steadily advanced metallurgy. Yet there was no "fallout" whatever to improve medieval society's most important tool, the plowshare. That had to wait until the eighteenth century.

Equally, there was no transfer from the civilian technology to the technology of warfare. In antiquity, the West knew only oared vessels. Between the eighth and tenth centuries north-western Europe converted both windmill and waterwheel into the first machines, that is, into the first tools of production that were not driven by human or animal labor; almost immediately the windmill sail was transferred to the seagoing vessel. But men-of-war remained oared galleys for another six or seven hundred years.

Then, in the seventeenth century, things changed drastically. For two hundred fifty years, through World War II, the defense economy and the civilian peacetime economy moved in tandem, mutually enriching each other. The turning point was the Dutch invention in the late seventeenth century of the first ship capable of carrying a substantial cargo in addition to its crew and their provisions. This ship, a man-of-war originally designed to carry heavy guns, was soon converted into the world's first efficient freight carrier. It was one of the greatest technological breakthroughs that peacetime economy ever experienced—as great a breakthrough as the steam engine or the computer or biotechnology. It brought about the commercial revolution of the eighteenth century in which, for the first time in history, trade was worldwide. Europeans started their march toward economic penetration and dominance of the entire globe. For two hundred fifty years almost every advance in military technology thus quickly provided new energy for the civilian economy. And civilian technology rapidly was applied to military technology. Military technology created the first modern roads, designed and built primarily for the attempt of Louis XIV of France to become master of the European continent in the early eighteenth century. They immediately became roads for inland trade. To provide the engineers to build the roads, the first technical university, the Ecole des Ponts et Chaussées, was founded (in 1747). With it emerged the profession of engineer and the systematic application of science and technology to the design and production of goods and services.

Conversely, every major innovation in the civilian economy during the two hundred fifty years after 1700 found military application almost immediately: the steam engine, the telephone, the wireless, the automobile, the airplane. And wars, for all their destruction and waste, provided economic impetus for two hundred fifty years, greatly speeding up technical developments that otherwise would have taken many decades to reach commercial application. The textbook example is Napoleon's paying for the forced-draft development of beet sugar to break Great Britain's monopoly on the supply of cane sugar to Europe; it is the first instance of "governmental defense research."

But for World War I, radio would probably not have been developed until thirty years later, that is, until the 1950s. Because of the poor performance of the field telephones during the battles of World War I, engineering talent and large quantities of government money were provided for the development of wireless transmission of voice and music. The computer might well have taken thirty or forty years longer but for World War II. The first working computer, the famous ENIAC, was built for military needs and with military money. The Cold War a few years later then gave IBM world leadership in computers. The military orders for "early warning systems" in the Canadian Arctic enabled IBM to design and manufacture the first working computers in substantial numbers.

Equally important: during the two hundred fifty years that began in the late seventeenth century, military and civilian production facilities were interchangeable. Civilian production facilities and civilian products could easily be converted to wartime production and wartime use, and could then be reconverted almost immediately to peacetime use. A major reason for Britain's surge into economic leadership in the early nineteenth century was its ability to convert the shipyards that had built Nelson's fleet to building the newly designed packet boats and clipper ships that came to dominate oceangoing trade for the next fifty years. This also happened on the other side of the Atlantic in the shipyards that had been built during the American Revolution and expanded during the War of 1812 to build an American navy. When the United States entered World War II in December 1941, it had literally no war production capacity. It took less than four months, however, to convert a plant that had been assembling Buick, Oldsmobile, and Pontiac automobiles in Linden, New Jersey, into the largest producer of carrier-based fighter planes. And by January 1946, five months after World War II had ended, the plant was again producing Buicks, Oldsmobiles, and Pontiacs.

But now this is over. Indeed, we now know that defense spending and defense technology are serious drains on the civilian economy. That the Japanese spend very little money on defense and even less on defense research and technology is, as everyone now admits, a major strength. In contrast, the heavy defense burden in the United States is a major—perhaps the major—cause of the loss of competitive strength and leadership of the American economy. The even larger portion of gross national product that goes into defense in Russia is surely one of the major causes for the backwardness and continuing deterioration of the Russian economy.

The main problem is people rather than money. Scientists and engineers do not work for the defense effort in Japan; they work for the civilian economy. In the United States as many as one third of the country's engineers are employed in defense work. Where their Japanese counterparts are likely to design a better-fitting door panel for the passenger car, the American technologist of similar competence is almost certain to be found working on tank design or "Star Wars." In Russia, competent scientists or technologists are altogether unlikely to be allowed to work for the civilian economy. They are drafted into defense work and stay there.

The growth of defense has become an even greater economic threat to the developing countries, and especially to Latin America. The burden of the military is the single biggest factor in these countries' economic stagnation, inflation, and lack of development. Defense spending in countries such as Peru, Chile, Argentina, or Brazil has probably absorbed half of the monies that otherwise would have been available for productive investment. The downfall of the Shah in Iran was caused, in large part, by the diversion of available foreign capital into building up what was, when the Shah fell, the largest single military force in the Near East (but one, as the war with Iraq showed, of no great military value).

The first economic priority must thus be to reduce and bring under control the defense spending and the diversion of high-grade human resources into economically unproductive—indeed, economically counterproductive—defense work.

No More School of the Nation

Socially, too, defense is rapidly becoming counterproductive. The French Revolution proclaimed the army to be the School of the Nation, and this soon became the slogan everywhere except in England and in the United States. It is still the slogan in Latin America. And it was the slogan of Mao's China. But whatever merit there ever was to this assertion, it no longer is valid. Military service may have inculcated the right habits when the recruits were illiterate peasant boys without skills, self-discipline, hygiene, or work habits. This is not today's population, even in the developing world. The much vaunted skills that a military teaches—the benefits of military service proclaimed by every recruiting poster—are only of the most limited value to the civilian economy. A year or two of community service for young people would have greater value both to them and to society than two years in the barracks.

On the contrary, the military has proven itself very much the wrong school for the civilian society. In one Latin American country after another the army took over when civilian government disintegrated—in Peru, in Chile, in Argentina, in Brazil. In every single case the takeover of government by the army was at first greeted with enthusiasm by a substantial majority of the population. In every single case army rule degenerated into tyranny, torture, corruption beyond anything seen before, and total ineffectualness within a year or two. So did army rule in Franco's Spain. The military "virtues" are simply not adequate to the demands of the modern world. Nor do they any longer—if they ever did—protect the military against the temptations of modern society and modern politics.

Military Aid and Political Malperformance

Military aid as a tool of policy is older than recorded history. Its results were always questionable. It was a Roman historian who remarked that a general who takes a subsidy will soon start looking for a higher bidder. Military aid is self-defeating not because generals are less trustworthy than other men but because dependence on outside support is a contradiction in terms for a military establishment. It is the task of the military to make its country *independent* and to keep it so. The more lavish the military aid from the outside, the more deeply it will be resented. The more successful and stronger the recipient grows, the more his objectives will diverge from those of the donor. Alliances against a common enemy work as long as there is a military threat. Military aid

51

as a tool of politics does not. It never has—as no less an authority than Winston Churchill repeatedly pointed out in his biography of his great ancestor, the Duke of Marlborough. Never before has military aid as a tool of policy been used as lavishly as in the forty years since World War II, and never before have the results been poorer. It is little consolation that the Russians were using it earlier than the West, more lavishly and with even poorer results, for example, in Yugoslavia or in China. In almost every case in which the United States tried generous military aid—the Greece of the Colonels, the Iran of the Shah, the Philippines of Marcos, or Noriega's Panama—it succeeded only in creating an enemy.

The most profound change, though, is the almost unrelieved record of military malperformance—by the military of all powers. For forty years now, most military actions have failed against any kind of opposition, even against small bands of guerrillas, terrorists, or saboteurs. Even where there was no or very little opposition, the results have not been impressive. The British threw the whole might of one of the world's largest navies and a well-trained army against an almost non-existing Argentine force in the Falkland Islands. It was a magnificent feat of logistics, but, as we now know, militarily close to fiasco. The Americans a few years later invaded tiny Grenada with a force of more than eight thousand men. They succeeded of course in occupying the island, especially as the native population greeted the Americans as liberators and saviors. But, as we now know, the operation was a near-disaster in military terms.

Whatever the causes, it is becoming clear that military forces are not militarily effective. One reason may be that even the mightiest country can prepare, plan, and train for only one kind of military action. With modern technology, however, there is an infinite number of possible military actions, each requiring different strategies, different tactics, different logistics, different training, and a different concept of warfare. Even more important, there are no central strategic concepts any more. There are only "options" and "contingencies," each equally probable or improbable. A force can be planned, trained, commanded, and equipped for one kind of warfare against one kind of enemy. It cannot be planned, trained, commanded, and equipped for any kind of warfare against any kind of enemy. A British fleet developed to guard the North Sea approaches against Russian submarines is the wrong force for convoying troopships in the remote South Atlantic. American destroyers built and equipped for naval battles in the open sea are singularly ill-equipped to shepherd tankers in the shallow, narrow Persian Gulf crowded with civilian, non-combatant air and sea traffic. As every writer on warfare has emphasized, from the ancient Chinese and Caesar to Clausewitz, tactics must be flexible. But strategy must be fixed, must be based on both clearly defined goals and unambiguous assumptions, and cannot be changed fast. Neither can training, command structures, or weapons.

Whatever the reason, the facts are clear: Arms no longer are capable of serving as the tool of policy. Paradoxically this explains, in large part, why arms production has grown so tremendously in the last forty years. We have tried to substitute mass for purpose. We have tried to regain the military potency of defense by making it gigantic, unwieldy, complex. It never works.

The Return of the Private Army

Governments are rapidly losing their monopoly on arms and their use—and this may well be the most ominous development. Since the modern state arose in the sixteenth century it has been axiomatic that it has to have a monopoly on warfare and on the means of warfare. There were still private armies in the Thirty Years' War that ravaged the European continent from 1618 to 1648. But all the European powers came out of that conflict with one clear policy: not to tolerate armies except under the control of the sovereign. This is what "defense" means: it is both the duty of the state to provide the means to defend the citizens against attack and the exclusive right of the state to do so.

This is still official doctrine. But is defense in this sense still possible? Is it indeed meaningful? President's Reagan's most controversial proposal was his Strategic Defense Initiative—or "Star Wars," as it soon came to be called. This proposal promised development of new technology to protect the United States against attack by nuclear weapons. Even if successful, Star Wars would not protect the United States against attack by nuclear weapons delivered by parcel post—and a very small parcel addressed to a post office box at the Empire State Building, whether mailed by a foreign government or a terrorist, would, if detonated by remote control, inflict more damage on New York City than the American bombing of Hiroshima and Nagasaki did in 1945. It would be even easier to bring in in a similar way—beyond any detection or defense—biological or chemical weapons of massive destructive power. The monopoly of the state on "defense" has been breached. The terrorist has reinstated the private army. There is no defense in the traditional sense against terrorism: the traditional military is impotent against it. Nor can it be controlled or stamped out by the action of any one government.

We have reached the end of the road that began with the "national state" four hundred years ago, the end of the road that led to national armies, national navies, national air forces, and to "defense" as a central core of national sovereignty and national policy.

Unilateral disarmament or pacifism is not the answer. Indeed, it has been the balance of deterrence, the "Mutually Assured Destruction" of nuclear war, which has kept the peace between the major powers during the last forty years.

There is great need now to stop the arms race. In that sense, the accord which President Reagan negotiated with the Soviet Union in the last year of his term, and which eliminates a whole class of nuclear weapons, is an important first step—but a first step only. What is needed above all is acceptance of the fact that to get rid of the arms race—and not just curtail it—is of equal interest to every single government in the world. The approach to disarmament for thirty years has been, "We will disarm if we get a military advantage." What makes the Reagan-Gorbachev treaty of 1988 important is that, tacitly, both sides agree that they have an equal interest in not gaining or maintaining an advantage. They have a common interest in becoming weaker militarily. But we are still a very long way from this being understood, let alone accepted. To accept that it is in the common interest of all countries to cut back on military expenditures and military establishment may, however, come easier than anyone would have thought only a few years ago. Economic necessity may force us to move in that direction. In every single major country except Japan the economy needs a sharp reduction in military spending: in the Soviet Union foremost, in China next, in the United States third. And in the developing countries the need is even greater. It would be the first time in human history that economic necessity has prevailed over military aggrandizement; but then it is also the first time in history that military aggrandizement is proving to be unproductive even in strictly military terms.

The time may even be approaching when all major nations can agree to forgo military aid as self-defeating and to band together to stop terrorism—as the nineteenth-century nations banded together in the Treaty of London of 1857 to stamp out piracy at sea, and as—at least tacitly—they agreed in the 1950s not to condone air piracy.

But the most important, the most fundamental need is reassessment of the function of defense and of arms altogether. "Defense" is no longer possible; only retaliation is. Arms are no longer an effective tool of policy. What does the military have to be, and how does it have to act, to be effective again?

PART II

GOVERNMENT AND
POLITICAL PROCESS

6

THE LIMITS OF GOVERNMENT

For almost two centuries, we hotly discussed what government *should* do. We almost never asked what government *can* do. Now increasingly the limits and function of government will be the issue. And government is no longer, as political and social theory still postulate, the only power center. In the developed countries both society and polity have become pluralist again, in startling reversal of the trends that prevailed since the end of the Middle Ages. These new pluralisms are very different from anything known earlier. The pluralism of society is one of apolitical, performance-focused, single-task institutions. The pluralism of the body politic is that of the new "mass movements": small, highly organized minorities, single-cause or single-interest in their focus, and totally political.

These new realities make new and different demands on political leadership. To try to satisfy them through "charisma," as so much popular discussion seems to ask for, can only result in misleadership and non-performance.

From Omnipotent Government to Privatization

Very few books in history have had greater impact than Adam Smith's *Wealth of Nations* (1776). It is still the one economics book that even the least educated have heard about. And yet Adam Smith's main point was virtually forgotten a few decades after the book had come out—and remained virtually forgotten until quite recently. Smith had little love for businessmen and even less for self-interest. He did *not* argue that government does a poor job running the economy. He argued that government, by its very nature, *cannot* run the economy, not even poorly. He did not, so to speak, agree that elephants are poorer flyers than swallows. He argued that government being an elephant can't fly at all.

But soon—no later than the end of the Napoleonic wars—the argument, even among Smith's followers, turned from what government *can* do to what government *should* do. Smith argued from the nature of government. The nineteenth century argued politics.

Even the most uncompromising advocates of the free market did not question government's competence in the nineteenth and twentieth centuries. They argued government's legitimacy. The most extreme opponent of government programs, government controls, and government activism in the late nineteenth century was the English philosopher Herbert Spencer, the last of the great Liberals. He even opposed public education as interference with personal liberty. Yet Spencer never questioned the ability of government to carry out programs. He denied government's legitimacy to do so. Similarly, the father of neoconservatism, F. A. Hayek, in his anti-government tract *The Road to Serfdom* (1944), did not argue government incompetence.*On the contrary, he viewed government as only too potent. He argued the threat to liberty

---

*Almost fifty years later, Hayek, in his 1989 book *The Fatal Conceit: The Errors of Socialism* (New York and London: Routledge)—published while *The New Realities* was at the printer's—came to the conclusion that the nature of information makes it impossible, both in theory and in practice, for government to manage or even to control the economy.

as the one compelling argument against government interference with the economy.

When the question of the limits of government was first raised two hundred years after Adam Smith's book, it was dismissed as irrelevant, if not as silly. As it happened, I was the first to do so, in my 1969 book *The Age of Discontinuity.* There I also coined the new term "privatization" for the divestiture by government of nationalized companies and industries which I anticipated. But when *The Economist* reviewed the book, it derided the very thought as perfect nonsense and as something that could not possibly happen.

Only eight years later Margaret Thatcher became prime minister of Great Britain and immediately started to privatize. Since then, privatization has not only become the program of Conservatives like Mrs. Thatcher in Great Britain or Jacques Chirac when he became prime minister of France in 1986. The French Socialists, regaining the prime ministership in France in 1988, vowed to continue privatization; indeed, they decided to privatize the biggest of all French nationalized industries, the Renault Automobile Company, despite stiff opposition from the labor movement. Privatization has become the official policy of Communist China. And it has been pushed furthest by a Labor government in New Zealand, which is even privatizing the postal service.

Another form of privatization is moving faster still: letting private contractors take over public services with governments paying them on the basis of competitive bids. First started in the 1970s in Minneapolis–St. Paul, Minnesota, by a political scientist and city administrator, Ted Kolderie, this practice has also spread worldwide. The state of Florida paroles criminals first sentenced to a jail term—about 25,000 at any one time—into the care of the Salvation Army. In many cities, even big ones, street cleaning, fire fighting, even police, are now "farmed out." Some American states have turned over running the prisons to private contractors. Even traditional "progressives" no longer doubt that there are limits to what government can do.

There are three reasons for this dramatic change. One is the failure of government programs and government operations since World War II. The second is that we have learned there are limits to what taxation and spending can achieve. Finally, we now know there are limits to government's ability to raise revenues.

What Can Government Do?

Most government activities of the nineteenth century worked beautifully. The Post Office, for instance, the nationalized railroads of Europe, the health-insurance programs of Imperial Germany, or workmen's compensation first developed in Imperial Austria around 1900 (with Franz Kafka, the great novelist, as one of its most competent administrators). The social programs of Franklin D. Roosevelt's New Deal in the 1930s were successes—at least there were very few failures.

But the only country in which government programs enacted after World War II have still been successful by and large is Japan. In every other country—and in democratic countries just as much as Communist ones—most post-World War II government programs have been disasters. If they achieved any results, these were often the very opposite of what they were enacted for. This goes for the frantic efforts in the Soviet Union since Khrushchev's day to improve farm production and farm productivity; when the Chinese, however, "privatized" their farms, production and productivity shot up almost overnight. But just as ineffectual was Lyndon Johnson's "War on Poverty" or the attempts of successive American administrations to stamp out drug abuse or to put welfare mothers to work.

Worse, the very programs and activities that did so well in the nineteenth century, and up to World War II, are now in deep trouble in most countries. Fred Smith, the founder and CEO of Federal Express, the multinational courier company, was asked in a meeting in Paris why his company does not operate in Switzerland. "It is the only Western country," he said, "in which the postal service still functions." The nationalized railroads of Europe are running horrendous deficits, as did the Japanese National Railroad before it was split up and privatized in 1986. Yet despite the enormous sums the taxpayers of Europe and Japan have been pouring into their railroads, only the non-governmental American railroads have remained effective freight carriers. No nationalized railroad in the non-Communist world carries more than one tenth of its country's freight. The American railroads carry two fifths—and make money doing so.

We now understand why there are some things government, by its very essence, cannot do. And even for the things government can do, conditions must be right. A government activity can work only if it is a monopoly. It cannot function if there are other ways to do the job, that is, if there is competition. The Post Office in the nineteenth century was a true monopoly. And so were the railroads. There were no other ways of sending information or of moving freight and people over land. But as soon as there are alternative ways to provide the same service, government flounders.

Governments find it very hard to abandon an activity even if it has totally outlived its usefulness. They thus become committed to yesterday, to the obsolete, the no longer productive. And government cannot give up either when an activity has accomplished its objectives. A private business can be liquidated, sold, dissolved. A government activity is "forever." There are now Sunset Laws which prescribe that government activities after a given time lapse unless they are re-enacted. But legislatures rarely refuse to renew an activity, no matter how obsolete or futile it has become. By that time it has become a vested interest.

Moral or Economic?

Above all, any government activity almost at once becomes "moral." No longer is it viewed as "economic," as one alternative use of scarce resources of people and money. It becomes an "absolute." It is in the nature of government activities that they come to be seen as symbols and sacred rather than as utilities and means to an end. The absence of results does not raise the question, Shouldn't we rather do something different? Instead, it leads to a doubling of effort; it only indicates how strong the forces of evil are. Economic matters are judged by a cost/benefit ratio. In moral matters, this is a dirty word, a "sellout," an "abandonment of principle." There are of course truly moral matters, in which any compromise is indeed betrayal. But even in a moral matter one should always question the effort if there are no results. By 1917, for instance, both the Germans and the Allies should have questioned the insane trench warfare of World War I with its fruitless human sacrifices. But by then the war had become moral for both sides, with "total victory" the only acceptable goal. This gave us communism in Russia, Hitler in Germany, the Great Depression, and World War II.

Drug abuse is horrible and an evil. But if after twenty years no results are achieved by governmental campaigns against it (and in the U.S. things are only getting worse), one might question the moral approach. It might be more productive then to do the one thing we can do: take the profits out of the traffic in drugs by eliminating criminal penalties on drug use—"immoral" though this sounds.

While drug abuse is indeed evil, and therefore a moral matter, electricity surely is economic. Yet in American politics today it is being treated as moral and a matter of principle. The Tennessee Valley Authority (TVA) long ago outlived the objective for which it was set up in the thirties: to provide cheap electric power to what was then a poor rural region.

The region is now neither poor nor rural; and the TVA's rates for electric power are among the highest in the nation. The whole system is in shambles. Yet when a new general manager recently dared to hint at privatizing it, there was a storm of outrage and moral indignation. What started as a utility and a tool to get cheap electricity had become a symbol, and "sacred."

Just as government can rarely abandon, it rarely innovates. Facsimile transmission does electronically and very fast what the Post Office has been doing very slowly by shipping heavy paper over great distances. Facsimile will probably be the Post Office of the future. But it has not been invented by the Post Office nor introduced by it.

Governments can do well only if there are no political pressures. The Post Office and the railroads did well as long as they had a simple purpose. But very soon, perhaps inevitably, the pressure builds to misuse such services to create employment, and especially employment for people who otherwise would find it hard to get jobs, for example, blacks in the U.S. Postal Service. And as soon as a governmental activity has more than one purpose, it degenerates.

Government services also will not perform if the basic assumptions under which they originated change. When workmen's compensation was introduced in the late nineteenth century, it was based on the assumption that industrial work is inherently dangerous. To be sure, workmen's compensation from the beginning aimed at encouraging employers to make work safer. Employers paid premiums based on their safety performance, which greatly encouraged them to improve their operations. But the basic assumption was still that industrial work, especially work around machinery, carries with it the risk of accident. Hence, workmen's compensation did not ask who was at fault. Its purpose was to make sure that the worker would be compensated no matter who or what was at fault. We no longer accept this assumption—except in

65

Japan (where, therefore, workmen's compensation still works well). In the West we assume that industrial operations should be safe. If there is an industrial accident, somebody is to blame—and this usually means the employer. Where workmen's compensation awards in the past were aimed at encouraging both employers and employees to improve safety, they now are seen as punishment. The result is distortion of the whole system, with expenses going up steadily and satisfaction and performance going down steadily.

These are stringent constraints on a government activity: that it remain the only way to do a certain task; that it not outlive its usefulness and not be continued once it has attained its objective; that it not be made to serve political ends, however laudable, but remain narrowly focused on specific performance for the public; and finally that the assumptions on which it is based remain unchanged. But these rules admit of no violation. The moment they are not being followed, the activity becomes "politicized." That invariably means fast degeneration of the service.

"Easy" Activities and "Hard" Activities

There also are activities that government cannot do well, and perhaps cannot do at all, even though they seem to meet all conditions for governmental effectiveness. Government will malperform if an activity is under pressure to satisfy different constituencies with different values and different demands. Performance requires concentration on one goal. It requires setting priorities and sticking to them.

Ted Kolderie who, as noted earlier, first advocated the farming out of municipal services to private contractors, talks of "easy" and "hard" government activities. Hard ones government cannot do, and certainly cannot do well. The difference between the two is in their politics. In an easy activity, all constituencies want the same performance—as they did with respect to the nineteenth-century Post Office. Activities are hard if different constituencies expect and demand different things and have different values and expectations. Most of the government programs since World War II—in the United States but in many other Western countries as well—either promised different things to different people or attempted to make one group in society benefit at the expense of another. Thus they became mired in controversy, and soon lost focus and the ability to perform. They were "hard" programs.

This distinction also explains why government-owned businesses will only work if run as moneymakers pure and simple, as were the Crown monopolies of the eighteenth century (the tobacco monopolies on the continent of Europe, for instance). Government-owned enterprises stop performing as soon as political or social values interfere with the single-minded pursuit of profit. They become hard. An example are the huge money-losing and mismanaged companies owned by the Italian government today and run in part as businesses, in part to employ workers, in part as patronage for politicians and their friends.

We are beginning to understand, though in crude outline only, the lessons of the post-World War II period in respect to government activities.

• There are functions that are clearly governmental which no one but government can be allowed to perform, and which only government can perform. Among them is the governmental monopoly on defense and arms. There is also the governmental function of maintaining law, order, and justice so that citizens can sleep peacefully at night and walk the streets without fear—something governments a century ago did a good deal better than most governments do today.

• There is a far more complicated and far more controversial government function: to maintain what we today call a "level playing field." Government can set ground rules that are equally binding on everybody. The Securities and Exchange Commission in the United States is effective precisely because it is in everybody's interest to have clear rules which enable the honest, whether buyers or sellers of securities, to do their business, and which keep out the crooks (or at least make it a little harder for them).

We know, in other words, that government can and should be a good deal more activist than the nineteenth-century Liberals such as Herbert Spencer preached and wanted. The role of government has to be much closer to the beliefs of the nineteenth-century Conservatives, who imposed limitations on government precisely because they wanted a strong and effective government.

• We know that not everything government does is forever. Yet to abandon a government activity is difficult and always bitterly resisted. Whatever government does always becomes "morality." Government activities therefore need to be organized as temporary from the outset. A new program, a new agency, should be enacted for a limited—and fairly short—period of time, with a clear statement of the results it is expected to achieve within that period, and with explicit commitment to abolishing it if it should fail to produce the promised results.

• Whatever non-governmental organizations can do better, or can do just as well, should not be done by government at all. What matters is not whether the activity is organized as a "business," with profit as an aim or at least as measurement. What matters is that it not be *run* by government. One way is privatization. Another way is to switch from government as a doer to government as the provider, with the work being done by outside contractors to government-set standards.

What Money Can't Buy

As important as the realization that there are limits to what government can *do* is the realization that there are limits to what government money can *buy*. In fact there are whole areas where spending government money can only make things worse. Can government money, for instance, change society—and how?

Compassion is a legitimate function of government, and so is the protection of the poor and oppressed. Government, the Old Testament prophets preached, should be a shepherd to its people. And the medieval king swore at his coronation to be "Father and mother to the poor." The most successful government programs in all history were programs to help the poor: the nineteenth-century "public works" to give the poor what only the very rich could afford in earlier times— sewers, clean water, public transportation, schools, medical care. These expenditures created, most successfully, an environment in which even the poor could hope to lead a decent life.

In the twentieth century we have been spending much larger sums of government money to change the social conditions of the poor. The results have been almost uniformly disappointing. And in some areas, the conditions of the poor have become worse as a result. The two worst fiascos among the government programs in the post-World War II period are two extremely expensive American ones: low-income housing and welfare. A good deal of the low-income housing the United States built at enormous cost has been abandoned. What's left is often worse than the slums it replaced: crime-ridden, fear-ridden, vandalized, dirty, rat-infested. And despite ever larger and constantly growing expenditures, the "welfare mess" in the United States is getting steadily worse. In fact, a strong case can be made—and has been made—that the poor in America, and especially the black poor, have become the poorer, the more helpless, the more disadvantaged, the more welfare money is being spent to help them. American welfare spending encourages dependence. It paralyzes rather than energizes.

In glaring contrast to these failures is what is probably the most successful government program of the last forty years: Prime Minister Thatcher's privatization of England's low-income public housing, the English council estates. Buying their flats turned renters into owners. Almost overnight both the spirit and the physical appearance of these slum tenements changed. They will never be an aesthetic delight. But they have become self-respecting, well maintained, and safe; they have become communities.

Should we abandon the idea of social change through government spending? Most of us would be reluctant to do so considering how great the needs are. But how much longer should programs be maintained that are unsuccessful and may well be doing harm rather than good?

What Taxes Cannot Do

Not even a further grace period should be given to the other, even less successful government attempt to change social conditions: the attempt to change income distribution through the tax system.

Oliver Wendell Holmes, the American legal scholar and judge, is widely remembered for his saying: "The power to tax is the power to destroy." But Holmes only put into a pithy phrase what had been known all along. Confiscatory and punitive taxes have a very long history. What was new and a product of Holmes's time was the idea that taxes could be used to reward. Taxes could be used to redistribute income, especially from the rich to the poor, and thus to further social justice and economic equality.

This was first proposed by Germany's "Academic Socialists" in the early 1900s. Opposed equally to capitalist exploitation and Marxist class war, these men—mostly economic historians—advocated income redistribution through the tax system as the "third way." It was an English politician, David Lloyd George, who then turned this into government policy in his budgets before World War I. After 1918 it became government policy everywhere. At the very time however that Lloyd George introduced his first budget, the Italian mathematical economist Vilfredo Pareto formulated what is known as Pareto's Law. After a lifetime of studying income distribution, Pareto concluded that government cannot effectively change the distribution of incomes. Modified only marginally by prevailing local customs and values, distribution is determined by the economy's productivity. The less productive an economy, the greater the inequality of incomes. The more productive, the less the inequality.

All our experience has validated Pareto's Law and has shown that the policy started by Lloyd George is ineffectual. To be sure, taxes can shift income and wealth. Lloyd George's inheritance tax has largely expropriated the very rich of 1900 England, the great landowners. But it has only shifted wealth to another group of the very rich—financiers, industrialists, businessmen. Insofar as Britain today is less unequal in respect to incomes and wealth than it was in 1900, it is so because it is far more productive. Because Britain today is however a good deal less productive than West Germany, its income distribution is a good deal less equal—despite a far more redistributive tax system. Inequality in Soviet Russia is probably as great as it is in Mexico—that is, very great. Officially there is, of course, egalitarianism in the Soviet Union. But as everybody knows by now, especially the Russians, the two million "bosses" in the *nomenclatura*—1 percent of the total population—enjoy perks of all kinds: special stores, special schools, special hospitals, special housing, special vacation dachas, reserved transportation, and so on. This gives them the standard of living and real income of the very rich. In Mexico similarly the very rich account for about 1 percent of the population. The Soviet Union and Mexico—in industry and agriculture—are today on roughly the same level of productivity. And only Pareto's Law can explain why income distribution in all developed countries is remarkably similar despite tremendous differences in tax rates and tax structure.

In fact only one governmental policy seems to be capable of changing the distribution of incomes and wealth: inflation. It expropriates the middle class. But it does so in large measure by destroying productivity.

Income redistribution through the tax system is still widely considered—by politicians as well as by voters—the most effective tool of social policy. But maybe the time has come to return to the old precept: the purpose of taxes is to produce revenue, and to do so with the fewest social and economic side effects.

The Limits of the Fiscal State

In the waning months of World War I, a great economist of the period, Joseph Schumpeter, published a short essay: *Der Steuerstaat (The Fiscal State)*. In it, Schumpeter, reflecting on the experience of the war, predicted a new era in government finance and government policy. Before World War I, he pointed out, there were no absolute governments. No government could raise, either through taxes or through borrowing, more than a very small percentage—perhaps 5 percent—of a country's national income. During World War I, however, every belligerent government raised, year after year, far larger sums—with the governments of the poorest belligerents, such as Austria and Russia, converting so much of their country's wealth into war bonds that their take in several years had been greater than the country's total income. This, Schumpeter predicted, would create a new and different economy in which inflationary pressures would become endemic. It would also, as he pointed out, undermine the political system. Since revenues had been limited throughout history, policy makers always had to make choices. They had to say no. With this limitation removed they would become unable to resist demands, especially if based on appeals to need or to conscience. Thus the ability of government to raise revenues would increasingly misdirect the flow of income from productive spending—for example, investment in wealth-producing facilities and new technology—into unproductive governmental spending aimed at redistributing income.

By now we know that Schumpeter was right. We also know that, contrary to Schumpeter, there are still limits. They are less restraining than the limits of a century ago. But they are real. There are limits to what government can actually raise. There are even narrower limits to what government can raise without damaging the economy seriously or undermining the cohesion of the body politic. The first to point this out, twenty years after Schumpeter, was an Australian economist, Colin Clark. Clark asserted, just before World War II, that government could not take more than around one quarter of a country's gross national product or gross personal income without creating irresistible inflationary pressures. Whether 25 percent is indeed the threshold, we do not know; the evidence would indicate that it might be closer to 40 percent. But there is such a limit. Above it, increased government revenue will not stimulate the economy. It will either depress it and create what we now call "stagflation," or it will create mounting inflationary pressures. And in all developed countries except Japan, the limit has been reached beyond which government expenditures become a threat and an affliction. Raising the share that government takes of the country's income above this threshold does not even produce increased revenue. Revenue may actually go down.

The Silent Tax Revolt

There is another, perhaps more serious restraint on the fiscal state. Once the government take, especially if collected through taxes, exceeds a certain percentage of gross national product or gross personal income—the figure seems to be around 35–40 percent or so—a silent but highly effective "tax revolt" starts. People stop working; what is the point if the additional income is being taxed away? Worse, people begin to cheat. In all countries in which the tax take approaches or exceeds 40 percent of gross personal income, a "gray economy" develops. In the United States there was almost no tax cheating before 1960. How big the gray economy in the United States has now become we do not know—there are of course no figures on it—but estimates range as high as 15 percent of the official economy. In countries like Sweden it is more like 30 percent. In Communist China, government economists put it at one third to one half of the total. In Italy, as everyone knows, the "gray economy" is the truly dynamic one—to the point that there have been labor shortages in Northern Italy for most of the last twenty years while the official statistics report unemployment ranging up to 20 percent. The same thing is happening in Spain. The official unemployment rate is well above 20 percent. Yet the figures for consumer spending would indicate an actual unemployment rate even below 10 percent.

Attempts to stamp out or even to curtail the gray economy are ineffectual as long as tax rates remain high. In fact, while everyone loudly condemns the gray economy, most people not only participate in it but consider it morally justified and even "clever." But this undermines the moral cohesion of society. It produces a dangerous political poison, cynicism. Seventy years ago Schumpeter warned that inflation would destroy free society (a warning he repeated twenty-five years later, in his 1942 book *Capitalism, Socialism, and Democracy*).

The post-World War I inflations in Europe, especially in Germany, amply bore out Schumpeter's warning. But the silent tax revolt of the gray economy is also a corrosive poison, albeit a slow one.

Are we thus at the end of the period in which government acknowledged no limits—either in respect to its activities, or in respect to its ability to change society, or in respect to its revenues? There are some first signs. At least politicians know that no one believes their promises any more. We may thus be approaching the end of the "spending state"—to paraphrase Schumpeter's term.

Will we again accept limitations on government's ability to raise money, whether by taxes or by loans? Will we learn to start again with the available resources in budgeting and in policy decisions rather than with the desirable expenditures? Will we again learn to say no? To make decisions is risky; it is indeed unpopular. But perhaps we are now ready to accept that to make decisions is what politicians are supposed to be doing.

7

THE NEW PLURALISMS

Both society and polity in developed non-Communist countries have become pluralist, each in a new and unprecedented way, and each also in a different way. Theory still postulates that there is only one organized power center—the government. But both society and polity in developed countries are now full of power centers that are outside of, and separate from, government. The new pluralism in society focuses on function and performance. It is a pluralism of single-purpose organizations, each concerned with one social task: wealth creation or schooling or health care or forming the values and habits of the young. This new pluralism of society is totally apolitical. The new pluralism of the polity by contrast focuses on power. It is a pluralism of single-cause, single-interest groups—the "mass movements" of small but highly disciplined minorities. Each of them tries to obtain through power what it could not obtain through numbers or through persuasion. Each is exclusively *political.*

Both the new pluralism of society and the new pluralism of the polity pose major challenges to political process and political leadership. The one because it is apolitical, the other because it is political to the exclusion of everything else.

The Pluralist Society

A hundred and fifty years ago social tasks were either not done at all or done primarily in the family, whether bringing up and educating children or taking care of the sick and old. Now social tasks are increasingly done in and through organized institutions—the business enterprise, the labor union, the hospital and the health-care system, the child-care center, the school, the university, and so on.

Seventy-five years ago practically all American babies were born at home; the maternity ward of the hospital was for the very poor or the very sick. Now almost all American babies are born in the hospital. Seventy-five years ago three quarters of American production came from family farms or from businesses employing fewer than five people. Now three quarters comes from businesses employing at least twenty-five people. And where seventy-five years ago the majority of American children still went to one- or two-room schools, the majority now attend consolidated schools with up to five or six thousand students in some high schools.

Each of these institutions is dedicated to a single task: producing economic goods or services as business does, constraining management's power within the enterprise as the labor union does; curing the sick; creating knowledge and disseminating it. They are single-purpose institutions. None of these institutions is a "government," or "political" (except the traditional European union). And yet each has to have a governing organ, a "management." Each has to have a great deal of autonomy to produce results. It makes little difference that one institution is legally independent (the private university or the non-governmental, non-profit private hospital in the U.S.) and another institution legally owned by the state and under the control of a government ministry (the universities and hospitals of Europe). And as even the Russians have learned, a business will perform—even poorly—only if run as an autonomous institution and, above all, as a *business,* whether privately owned or nationalized. The totalitarianism of the 1920s and 1930s—in Russia, Italy, and in Germany— can be seen as last attempts to maintain the central government's monopoly on power by embracing and subordinating all of society, all social institutions, all social functions. But totalitarianism, whether of the right or left, failed—and not only in creating a viable new society. It failed miserably in its attempt to snuff out the autonomy of the new institutions. All the totalitarians can do is to smash them—as Mao's China did, quite successfully, during the "Cultural Revolution." Neither the Russians, nor the Nazis, nor the Fascists, nor Mao's Chinese succeeded in running them. To get any results, they had to restore a substantial measure of autonomy to them.

Each pluralist institution serves a specific, limited function. This narrow focus is its greatest strength. Whenever an institution tries to go beyond its specific concern, it immediately loses effectiveness. The best example is the American school. However necessary, even desirable, it might have been to make the American school the engine of racial desegregation, it weakened the school's ability to do its first job: to teach children, whether black or white.

The new institutions are not based on power. They are based on *function.* Yet while non-political—indeed, apolitical—each institution has to have a considerable degree of power over people—power to hire, to place, to move, to fire; power to assign tasks to people; power to set performance standards and enforce discipline; power over working hours. Increasingly these institutions provide the individual in developed countries with livelihood, career, and opportunity to contribute, to achieve, to be productive. A hundred or a hundred and fifty years ago most people were still on the farm, tilling a few acres with no help other than their families. Most craftsmen then worked for themselves or with a hired man or two, as did practically all professionals. People who were employed worked for a "master" or "mistress." Except for soldiers, clergymen, and teachers—very small groups a century ago—hardly anyone worked for an "institution." Few had a "boss." The largest single group of employees a hundred years ago were domestic servants, even in the most highly industrialized countries. In 1910 domestic servants still formed more than one third of the English labor force; and even the United States was not far behind. Most domestics worked as personal subordinates for middle-class or working-class families who had one servant, or at most two, with "master" and "mistress" economically not very much better off than maid or cook.

When Marx wrote, a hundred and twenty years ago, the "proletarian" also worked for a "master" rather than for an organization. The best picture of the nascent industrial society of a century ago can be found in the novel *The Princess Casamassima,* by the great American writer Henry James, written in 1886, three years after Marx's death. It tells of an anarchist conspiring to bring about The Revolution by assassinating an important "imperialist" personage. The book's "exploited proletarians"—its hero and anti-hero, respectively—are highly skilled craftsmen, one working for a bookbinder employing eight people, the other for a manufacturing chemist employing fewer than twelve. And these capitalist employers were hardly much better off than the "exploited proletarians" in their pay.

By contrast, the great majority of all people in developed countries today work in and for an organization. Domestic servants, the largest employee category a hundred years ago, have practically disappeared in developed countries. No more than 3 to 5 percent of the population in any developed country make their living as full-time farmers, even though farm production today is many times what it was a hundred years ago in every non-Communist developed country. The center of population gravity are now "employees," not "workers"; indeed, the manufacturing worker, the heir of Henry James's "proletarian," is on the way to joining domestic servants and farmers in the limbo of history. In numbers, manufacturing workers have shrunk to one sixth of the labor force in developed non-Communist countries and will have shrunk further to one tenth or less of the total by the end of this century. The new workforce, while "knowledge workers" rather than "blue collar," are however all "employees"—not of a master but of an organization. Increasingly in all developed countries it is the most highly educated and the most highly paid who are employees. In fact, more than nine out of every ten people with a higher education in developed societies can expect to spend all their working lives as employees in an organization.

When Did It Start?

This new pluralism is almost the opposite of what anybody, only a hundred years ago, could possibly have imagined. For five hundred years, from the fourteenth century through the nineteenth, the central objective of political action and political thought was to abolish autonomous institutions within society, and to concentrate power in the hands of central government. Whatever their differences, princes and governments for five hundred years all agreed on this goal, and so did political philosophers. It was what "sovereignty"—a sixteenth-century term—meant. The process began with the step-by-step subjection of feudal lords and independent knights whose castles could not withstand gunpowder. It ended during and after the French Revolution with the abolition of all privileges: of the Church, of the universities, of the guilds, of the remaining free cities. What was left by 1850 were ceremonial remnants without power or meaning—the Lord Mayor of London riding in a magnificent glass coach to his inauguration into a powerless office. By the middle of the nineteenth century actual power was in the hands of a government, whether limited as in the West or supposedly "unlimited" as in the Czar's Russia. Giving this development its appropriate theory, the English jurist John Austin asserted that law is only what emanates from the central authority of the state, whether through legislation or through the law courts. There is neither "natural law" nor "custom." But there are also no limits on the power of the state, no countervailing powers. Austin was echoed, a few years after his death, by the most influential legal philosopher of the century, Sir Henry Maine—also an Englishman—who to universal acclaim announced in 1861 that the "historical progress of the law" has been "from status to contract." In modern society, according to Maine, there are only individuals. No saying was more widely quoted in mid-Victorian society than Maine's epigram.

But at the very time that "sovereignty" thus triumphed, a truly new power center arose, the modern business enterprise—the large railroad in the United States, and the so-called universal bank in Germany. Business, in one form or another, had been around for centuries. Yet the new business of the late nineteenth century was different from anything seen before—and much bigger. In two of Charles Dickens's most popular novels—*Nicholas Nickleby* (1838–39) and *Dombey and Son* (1846–48)—businesses are at the very center. But the great banking house of Dombey and Son which comes to such an ignominious end consisted of an owner, a general manager (the villain of the tale), and two clerks. There are two businesses in *Nicholas Nickleby.* One is a villainous moneylender who employs one alcoholic clerk. The other is the almost saintly firm of the Brothers Cheeryble, the leading merchants in the Baltic trade, consisting of the two brothers who own the business and their one upright clerk. Nor were the businesses that Dickens's contemporaries, Honoré de Balzac in France and Gustav Freytag in Germany, depicted in their tales any different. The new businesses were thus a tremendous shock; and the shock persisted for a long time.

America's leading labor economist in the first half of the twentieth century, John R. Commons, in *Legal Foundations of Capitalism* (1924), could explain modern business only as the result of a "conspiracy" by the Justices of the Supreme Court. But the modern business developed, of course, just as much in countries that had no Supreme Court, whatever their legal system: in Germany, Great Britain, France, Japan, and Russia. Though thus obvious nonsense, Commons's book was treated with tremendous respect and enjoyed wide popularity. The German Walther Rathenau, the first Western writer on the modern corporation as a social institution—and himself the head of one of the earliest large multinationals, the (German) General Electric Company (AEG)—felt similarly uneasy about the new phenomenon. So did his Japanese counterpart, Shibusawa Eiichi, statesman, Japan's premier banker, and founder of one of the earliest business schools, the present Hitsosubashi University.

That the first new power center was the business corporation explains why we still hear the word *"business* management" whenever anyone says "management." It explains why for almost a hundred years the discussion has focused on the relationship between business enterprise and government, business enterprise and labor, business enterprise and the community. It explains why we talk primarily of the "social responsibilities of business" rather than of the "social responsibilities of modern organizations."

The second of the new pluralist institutions actually developed only a few years after business: the modern civil service. It started to grow, both in power and size, around 1875 or 1880. The new civil service resembled its forerunners just as little as the corporate business giants of today—Citibank, IBM, Siemens, Sony—resemble Dickens's Brothers Cheeryble. What the traditional civil service looked like is vividly portrayed in *Orley Farm* (1862), one of the most successful of Anthony Trollope's novels. A central chapter takes place in the Home Office—then Britain's most powerful department of state. The Home Office employed six people—the minister, who was a member of parliament and a politician; the permanent secretary; and four clerks. Nor was the ministry over which Karenin, the powerful bureaucrat and hapless husband, presides in Leo Tolstoy's *Anna Karenina* (written in 1875–77) any larger, though the Czar's Russia was already notorious at that time for its "swollen bureaucracy." Since the modern civil service began, one new pluralist institution after the other has arisen and has grown in function, size, prominence, and power: labor unions; schools and universities (with their explosive growth after World War II); the whole health-care system; the enormous machinery of the welfare state; the "third-sector," non-profit institutions in the United States; and many others.

Pluralism is nothing new. Indeed, most societies throughout history were pluralistic. But there is a crucial difference between any earlier pluralism and the present one. All earlier pluralisms were based on *power*. The present one is based on *function*. In traditional Western pluralism king ranked duke, duke ranked count, count ranked knight, and knight ranked yeoman. Each exercised power over the next-lower level. And each exercised power within his own domain. But the power of each rested ultimately on the same source: control of land. Each ultimately had the same concern: to wrest a livelihood from the soil. Even in that small island in the rural ocean, the medieval city, the pluralist institutions all attempted to be complete communities and to exercise political control. The craft guilds—the weavers in fifteenth-century Florence, or the goldsmiths in the London of Elizabeth a hundred years later—forced their members to live in the same quarter of the city and to have their shops there, too. They dictated how many apprentices and how many journeymen each member could have, which of the journeymen could become a "master" and on what conditions. They regulated the prices their members paid for raw materials, the prices they charged for their goods, and the wages they paid. Each guild had its own church and usually reserved the priests' job in it for the son of a member. Just as the count and the knight tried to gain control of the courts in their domains, the guilds tried to take over the administration of justice within their membership.

By contrast the new pluralist organization of society has no interest in government and governance. Unlike the earlier pluralist institutions, it is not a "whole." It is an "organ" of society. As such, its results are entirely on the outside. The "product" of a business is a satisfied customer. The "product" of the hospital is a cured patient. The "product" of the school is a student who ten years later puts to work what he or she has learned. On the inside there are only costs.

In some ways the new pluralism is thus far more flexible, far less divisive than the old pluralism. The new institutions do not encroach on political power as did the old pluralist institutions, whether medieval church, feudal baron, or free city. The new institutions, however, unlike the old ones, do not share identical concerns or see the same world. Each of the new institutions perceives its own purpose as central, as an ultimate value, and as the one thing that really matters. Tunnel vision is always the degenerative disease of specialists, the price they pay for "professionalism" and for their narrow focus. The old institutions, the counts, the dukes, the barons, the abbeys, the bishops, and the free cities, constantly wrangled over precedence and rank. But they did not have the slightest difficulty understanding each other. No one ever talked about "communications." Today, no hospital administrator worries whether he or she "ranks" the corporation vice president or the chairman of the university's psychology department. But they constantly worry about communications. Every new institution speaks its own language, has its own knowledge, its own career ladder, and, above all, its own values. Not one of them sees itself as responsible for the community as a whole. That is somebody else's business. But whose?

The Position of the Individual

Equally new is the position of the individual. And it is equally incompatible with what political and social theory still sees as "normal." The nineteenth century had two competing models of society. One foresaw a society composed of small independents: the farmer with his forty acres and a mule, the small shopkeeper, the craftsman. They would all be equals. None of them would have power or wealth, but none would be abysmally poor or dependent either. Though he had his counterparts in every European country, Thomas Jefferson in the United States formulated this ideal most clearly. By the time Jefferson died in 1826, it had already become clear that society was not going his way. Out of this disenchantment arose the counter-utopia which found its final and clearest expression in the Marxian prophecy of a society consisting of an enormous mass of equally impoverished, equally exploited, equally dependent proletarians, totally dominated by a mere handful of capitalist exploiters.

Neither prophecy has become reality. The reality is something that neither Jefferson nor Marx—nor indeed anyone before 1950 or 1960—could have imagined: a society of "knowledge employees" who are neither exploited nor exploiters; who individually are not capitalists but who collectively own the means of production through their pension funds, their mutual funds, their savings; who are subordinates but often also bosses themselves. These people are both independent and dependent. They have mobility. But they also need access to an organization—as "consultants" if not as "employees"—to have any effectiveness at all.

The new pluralism often transcends traditional geographic boundaries. Business was the first of the new pluralist organizations to do so. It became "multinational" as early as 1860 and 1870. But other institutions are rapidly following suit. Accounting firms and law firms have already done so, as have consulting firms. Even universities are now becoming "transnational." And this too is incompatible with the political theories that still dominate our thinking, our teaching, and our legal approaches.

If history is any guide, it will take a century or so before we have legal and political doctrine appropriate to the realities of the new pluralism. But we cannot wait until the philosophers explain theoretically what has happened. Politicians, law courts, businessmen, executives of the new organizations have to act.

In five areas the new pluralism already challenges us:

- the social responsibility of the pluralist institutions;
- their community responsibility;
- their political responsibility;
- the individual's rights and responsibilities;
- the role and function of government in a pluralist society.

What Does Social Responsibility Mean?

There is one question the new pluralism raises to which we do know the answer—not in specifics, maybe, but in principle. We know in rough outline the social responsibility of the pluralist institutions of society. We know that their first social responsibility is to do their job. We know secondly that they have responsibility for their impacts—on people, on the community, on society in general. And finally we know that they act irresponsibly if they go beyond the impacts necessary for them to do their own job, whether it is taking care of the sick, producing goods, or advancing learning.

That the pluralist institution's first responsibility is to discharge its own specific function may sound obvious. It is, however, all too often forgotten in today's discussions and needs constantly to be emphasized. Whenever a "social responsibility" of any of these institutions—the university, the business, the labor union, the hospital—is being invoked, the first question has to be: Will it impair the institution's capacity to perform? We may well decide that the social good outweighs the cost of the sacrifice in performance. But it is dangerous, it is indeed irresponsible, not to ask the question or to pretend that it is irrelevant—which is what we did in the United States when we decided to make the school the agent of racial desegregation. Had we then asked the question, we would almost certainly still have desegregated the schools. The great sin of segregation and racial discrimination had to be corrected, had to be expiated. But we might have found ways to avoid, or at least to contain, the damage to the capacity of the school to teach. We might, for instance, have started with experimental programs in a few schools selected for their high standards and their strict discipline. By brushing aside as racist and irrelevant all questions regarding the school's primary task, we only assured that we got neither desegregation nor scholastic achievement.

Every one of the pluralist institutions, whether business or university or hospital, has impacts. It has to exercise considerable control over the people who work for it; otherwise, it cannot do its job. It has considerable impact on people who are customers, whether they buy a company's goods or are patients in a hospital. And it has impacts on bystanders. The factory that closes at four-thirty in the afternoon creates a traffic jam for everyone in the community. Responsibility for one's impacts is the oldest principle of the law. It does not matter whether the institution is at fault or is negligent. The Roman lawyers who first formulated this principle called it the "doctrine of the wild animal." If the lion gets out of its cage, its keeper is responsible. Whether the lion's keeper was careless and left open the door of the cage, or whether an earthquake released the lock, is irrelevant. By its very nature a lion is ferocious. By its very nature every one of the new pluralist institutions has impacts for which it is responsible.

We often hear the complaint these days, especially in the United States, that liability suits, malpractice suits, environmental suits, and their high damage awards want to make the universe "riskless." No doubt many of these suits are frivolous and many of the awards outrageous. But the basic assumption underlying these actions is not that the universe ought to be riskless. On the contrary, these suits are based on the recognition that there are new and very real risks—the man-made impacts of the new institutions. There has to be insurance against such risks; and the only way, so far, is to hold the institution responsible as the "keeper of the wild animal."

This means then that the institution has a duty—but also a self-interest—to limit its impact to what is actually needed for the discharge of its social function. Anything that goes beyond this is illegitimate and usurpation of power. Let me exemplify: American courts draw a sharp line between two provisions in the employment contract that to businessmen seem to be almost identical. The courts are reluctant to enforce restrictions on the freedom of former managerial and professional employees to go to work for a competitor. At the same time the courts have become exceedingly strict in forbidding ex-employees to lure customers away from their former employer, or to betray trade secrets to a new employer. Restricting the mobility of an employee is seen by the courts as going well beyond what is needed for a firm to do its job. It is not a necessary exercise of power, and is thus illegitimate. But to lure away customers or to betray trade secrets is a breach of trust and does damage to the former employer. To guard against such behavior is legitimate. It is a necessary impact.

It is this distinction between impacts that are necessary and those that are not which explains why few people so far worry greatly about the monopoly the university has on the degree. In the knowledge society, denial of a degree bars access to jobs, careers, and livelihoods. This is power far beyond what any other pluralist institution exercises. The university therefore is expected to observe due process in exercising this power. But it has to have the degree-granting power to discharge its function. By contrast the power of a labor union to deny access to a craft or a job is increasingly considered illegitimate and an abuse of power. The consequences are actually less severe than the denial of a degree; there is usually alternative employment for the individual worker. But the labor union does not truly need monopoly power over access to craft and job to perform its function. Most institutions justify as "benevolent" activities that go beyond the impacts necessary for the discharge of their function. The labor union "protects" its members when it keeps out what it considers "undesirables" (e.g., blacks in the American construction unions). The company is "paternalist" when it forces its workers to live in company-owned housing (in Japan, with its extreme housing shortage, this is actually still a "benefit"). All institutions like to think that they protect "standards," "quality," and "credentials." But unless an impact is clearly necessary to, and inherent in, the institution's function, this assumption is usurpation of power. Even if the impact is necessary—if it does damage, environmental damage or damage to health, for instance, the institution is responsible.

Community Responsibility

Should pluralist institutions take responsibility for community problems that are not of their own doing, social problems for instance—and if so, to what extent? In the 1960s the mayor of New York City called on the city's large businesses to take care of unwed black welfare mothers. New York at that time was on the verge of social disintegration, with employer after employer fleeing a city in which crime and drug addiction were rampant and city services collapsing. There was urgent need for effective action and no one around to take it, except the large and rich corporations headquartered in the city. Yet the mayor was soundly ridiculed by everyone. Not one company heeded his call. Crime and drug addiction were even more rampant in New York twenty years later than they were in the sixties; the city services had become even worse. Yet New York City experienced a virtual renaissance in the 1980s, brought about by the architectural revival of both downtown and midtown Manhattan. New office buildings transformed the city physically and aesthetically. This then brought back business, brought back tourists, restored the economy, and fueled a cultural upsurge, especially in art and art museums.

Another example: in the war on drug abuse, the lead has been taken by the Boy Scouts and Girl Scouts of America. In their work with elementary schoolchildren—and one out of every four of them in the United States is a Scout—the two organizations try hard, with considerable success, to inculcate resistance to drugs well before the children are actually exposed to the menace.

The first thing these examples teach—and it may be the most important lesson—is that most of the discussion of community responsibility misses the point. Most of it follows New York's mayor of twenty years ago in demanding that the pluralist institutions—and especially businesses, of course—rush in to take care of whatever social problems a community suffers from. "If the business, the labor union, the hospital, the university are so big, so strong, so professional, so competent, why can't they take care of poverty, of ignorance, of the schools?" But there is another, though much smaller, group

which agrees with the American Nobel Prize-winning economist Milton Friedman that the pluralist institutions should
stay out of anything that is not strictly and narrowly their
function. "It is difficult enough," Friedman would say, "for
business to do a decent job as a business. It is untrue to its
social responsibilities if it concerns itself with anything but
producing goods and services customers want, and generat-
ing the profit needed to form the capital for tomorrow's risks,
investments, and growth."

Both positions are right and both are wrong. The pluralist
institutions are in the community. They cannot, as the Benedictine monks of pre-medieval Europe tried to do, retreat into
isolation when the world around them goes to pieces. But
they also cannot—indeed must not—act beyond their narrow
competence and in defiance of their own specific function.

In the early years of this century a Chicago clothing mer-
chant, Julius Rosenwald, took over an ailing mail-order house
called Sears, Roebuck. Within ten years it had become the
world's largest and most profitable retailer. One reason was
Rosenwald's recognition that to prosper, Sears needed a
healthy farm community. But the American farmer at the
beginning of the century was in desperate straits, dirt-poor,
isolated, backward in his technology, with little access to education and even less to modern farming methods. Yet there
was an enormous amount of agricultural technology available, the result of well over a hundred years of research and
experimentation. Rosenwald invented the Farm Agent to act
as the change agent on the American farm. He financed this
new institution himself for ten years until it had become so
successful that the U.S. government took it over. By then the
farmer had acquired enough competence and purchasing
power to buy from Sears. Milton Friedman, had he been con-
sulted, would have told Rosenwald to stick to business and
leave concern for the farmer to the government. In other

words, community responsibility that is concern for a healthy and viable community is not "philanthropy" for the pluralist institution. It is self-interest.

Such community responsibility works, though, only under stringent conditions. It must fit the institution's competence. It must fit its value system. It must be an extension of what it is doing rather than a diversion. In that sense Friedman is right. If any business in New York City had followed the mayor's advice in the 1960s, it would only have done harm to the community. It would have been totally irresponsible. Business restored New York because real-estate development fits its values, its visions, its competence. Social work does not.

Similarly when the American hospital went into the inner-city health clinic, it did so with the best of intentions—but without much by way of results. The basic problems of the inner-city "underclass" are social problems: inadequate housing, lack of jobs, lack of knowledge and motivation. These problems hospitals cannot tackle. But health, the hospital's concern and value, never has been a priority of the very poor. And even in desegregating the schools, the United States succeeded—although very late—with the "magnet school" for achieving students. The magnet school stresses education as central. It therefore fits the values of teachers and the expectations of students. In such a school, white teachers respect black students because they learn; white students respect black teachers because they teach; white and black students respect each other because both achieve. And black students—perhaps the most important result—respect themselves, because they are achieving students. The best way to discharge a community responsibility is by making it serve the institution's primary task.

Political Responsibilities

The central question in every pluralism has always been: Who takes care of the common good? The traditional answer—it goes back hundreds of years—is self-delusion. The common good, it asserts, will emerge out of the welter and clash of conflicting interests. This at best produces stalemate. What is needed is for pluralist institutions to build into their own vision, their own behavior, and their own values concern and responsibility for the common good. They need to take political responsibility.

There are a few examples. Big business in post-World War II Japan organized itself to build political responsibility into its decision-making process, while successfully pursuing its own business interests. The large Japanese companies (in sharp contrast to their attitude in the twenties and thirties) learned not to start out with the question: What is good for business? but with: What is good for Japan? And then they asked: How should business pursue its own interests so that it serves the common good? Japanese business, in the period of the country's reconstruction, started out with its political responsibility. And this, rather than control by bureaucrats, was the real "Japanese secret." Something similar went on in West Germany during the same period. For thirty-five years after World War II, the big banks tended to think through industrial policy by starting with the question: What does the German economy and German society require?

These, however, were short-lived exceptions. In both Japan and West Germany, the political responsibility of business has all but disappeared since both countries recovered from defeat and destruction. So has the political responsibility that some of the European labor unions—the Dutch, for instance—assumed after World War II. Unless institutions learn, however, to ask what the community requires, they will increasingly lose public support, as have the labor unions in the United States and Great Britain. The American hospital is in crisis too in large part because it failed to take political responsibility, and with it leadership, in controlling costs and quality of health care. Political responsibility is thus the self-interest of the pluralist institution.

The Individual's Rights and Responsibilities

In earlier pluralist societies, individuals were expendable. The institution did not depend on them. Whether peasants or workers, individuals had no bargaining power; to quote Marx, they were the "industrial reserve army" and industrial cannon fodder. The new pluralist institutions of society are, however, organizations of "knowledge workers." Knowledge workers have mobility. They are "colleagues." They have both social and economic status. They enjoy the bargaining power that results from social equality and from being economically essential. Thus we will have to think through and redefine both the rights and the responsibilities of the knowledge worker in pluralist society and in its institutions.

The job of the individual will become a property right. We have, in fact, already gone quite far in that direction. American courts now regularly hold that employees, and especially managers, professionals, and technologists, have a right in their job even if there is no specific contract or tenure. This right can only be diminished or taken away by dismissal for specific reasons and with "due process." The courts hold, in other words, that the job has to be treated as a species of property. This is not "radical," but a conservative position. Whatever gives access to livelihood, status, and position in society has been considered property, since the Roman lawyers more than two thousand years ago first defined the term.

For the great majority of people in developed societies, and especially for the overwhelming majority of educated men and women, access to a livelihood requires a job in one of the new pluralist institutions. For the great majority the job also defines their position in society. The only access most people have to a little capital and financial independence is through the pension fund of the institution that employs them. For the great majority, in other words, property is what the job provides, if not the job itself. Every employing institution can therefore expect that it will be able to deprive people of their jobs only if it observes the rules that have always governed property. To deprive anyone of his or her job—or to diminish it—the institution must act according to pre-set standards, especially standards of performance. These must be uniformly applied and must be public. And increasingly, the employer will have to bear the burden of proof that it judges and rewards people against these standards. The employer will also have to satisfy requirements of "due process" in depriving individuals of their job or even in diminishing their job, for example, through a demotion, a cut in salary, perhaps even a job assignment that represents a cut in status and position. This means formal warning, proper review, and the right to appeal.

At the same time—in sharp contrast to the position of the individual in any earlier pluralism—the individual will have the right to move freely. Even in Japan, despite the tradition of "lifetime commitment," knowledge workers now have increasing mobility as long as they observe ritual courtesies. The employer rather than the employee is committed—as befits the shift in their respective bargaining power. The knowledge worker needs a job, to be sure. But only in a genuine and long-lasting depression does the knowledge worker need a job more than the employer needs the knowledge worker.

This is the lesson that hostile takeovers, divestitures, consolidations, leveraged buyouts, and the other financial manipulations of the last ten or fifteen years have taught America's knowledge workers. When large numbers of them suddenly found themselves out of a job, many after years of service with the same company, it was a tremendous shock at first for most of them. Then, almost without exception, even people in their mid-fifties found new jobs within a few months. In a good many cases the new job was better than the one they had lost. They found that knowledge gives them mobility—a lesson unlikely to be forgotten.

The rights of the employee—the job as a species of property and the right to mobility—must not impair the institution's ability to do its job, however. They must not impair its ability to abandon, to retrench, to enforce discipline and performance standards. An example of what not to do are the employment laws of Belgium and Holland. To protect workers, both countries impose heavy penalties on laying people off. All that this has done is to create record unemployment and economic stagnation. Employers forgo expansion rather than hire new people. Similarly, the absolute job security regardless of the performance of enterprise or employee that both Soviet Russia and Communist China give to employees is a major cause of their countries' economic backwardness and of their miserable living standards.

But what about the responsibilities of the individual? So far, that question has hardly even been asked. Since knowledge workers have considerable power, they must also assume responsibility. Their sole responsibility—and the one most sadly lacking today—is responsibility for the individual's own contribution. It is not enough for the knowledge worker to apply his or her knowledge; that knowledge must be applied so that it redounds to joint performance. This requires that knowledge workers direct themselves toward the objectives of the institution. The professional specialist however tends to be ever more specialized. By itself, specialized knowledge has no results unless it focuses on the needs and goals of the entire organization. The flute part is an essential part of a Beethoven symphony, but by itself it is not music. It becomes music by being part of the "score," by becoming an input that joins together with the inputs of sixty-five other musicians and their instruments. Similarly, what the market researcher produces in a business, the X-ray technician in the hospital, the historian in the university, is "input" only until it is focused on a common objective and put into a common task with the input of others. The more knowledge-based an institution becomes, the more it depends on the willingness of individuals to take responsibility for contribution to the whole, for understanding the objectives, the values, the performance of the whole, and for making themselves understood by the other professionals, the other knowledge people, in the organization.

The Role of Government

What role does government have to play in this pluralist society and *vis-à-vis* its pluralist institutions? This is clearly an important issue—it may be the most important one. Yet we do not even know the right questions. One reason for our confusion is that there are no precedents in history. The new institutions of pluralism are apolitical. With the exception of the labor unions, they have nothing but contempt for political values and the political process. Mussolini's Italy, seventy-five years ago, attempted to create a third house of parliament to represent the institutions: business, labor, the universities, and so on. Even people who had no use for fascism—Herbert Hoover in the United States, George Bernard Shaw in England, German and French Socialists—thought this an excellent idea. It was a complete fiasco.

He who pays the piper calls the tune, says the old proverb. Many of the new institutions are financed, at least in part, by government and out of tax money. The civil service depends entirely on government money. So do health care, education, the universities—even the churches—in most countries. Even in the United States, tax money pays for more than one third of health care and for three quarters of all schools, from kindergarten through graduate school. Yet governmental budget power is at best a crude weapon. It can impose a specific change in this or that practice. It can force American hospitals to shift to specific diagnoses to get reimbursed for treating old people. It can force Oxford and Cambridge universities to change their tenure rules. But the patient in an American hospital will still be treated the way hospitals have always treated patients. Oxford and Cambridge will still appoint and pick the scholars they want for their faculties, and treat their students the way they think students should be treated. And the one institution that most depends on government for its income, the civil service, is least amenable to political direction.

These institutions do indeed have to be apolitical and outside of the political process in order to function and to perform. They must not be politicized but be governed by their own values. "Education is much too important to be left to politicians," every schoolmaster will say. "Health care is much too important to be left to politicians," every physician and hospital administration will say. "Productivity is much too important to be left to politicians," every businessman will say. And the civil service in every country says the same thing about policy making. Each institution is right from its own vantage point. And yet education, health-care productivity, and policy making are political matters of the first magnitude. Every government is held accountable by its people for the performance of these institutions. It has a responsibility but it does not have much authority. What then can or should government do?

We know that government can set limits, especially when an institution becomes arrogant. Franklin D. Roosevelt did that in the 1930s with respect to American business and Margaret Thatcher in the 1980s with respect to both England's labor unions and its ancient universities. Perhaps the most

important future task of government in a pluralist society is to set standards. What should, what could a country expect from these new, powerful, autonomous institutions on the values and performance of which both the nation's and the citizen's well-being increasingly depend?

The Tyranny of the Small Minority

The pluralist institutions of society focus on one single task. The new pluralist groups in the polity are concerned with a single *cause.* It may be to save wildflowers or to ban abortion; to prevent regulation and restriction of firearms, the aim of the National Rifle Association in the United States; to prevent any cut in the subsidies to farmers in Brittany or to American tobacco growers; or to stop modern retailers such as supermarkets in Japan. That the cause is unpopular does not matter. The single-cause group derives its power from being a minority, and usually a very small one. Its strength lies in its single purpose rather than in numbers. Its task is almost never to get something done. It is to stop, to prevent, to immobilize. This is the new "mass movement" that increasingly dominates political process.

Sigmund Freud was highly controversial from his earliest days, but only one of his innumerable critics attacked him for choosing the wrong *question.* Almost sixty years ago a very young and still totally unknown Viennese writer, Elias Canetti—eventually, in 1981, to receive the Nobel Prize in Literature—sharply criticized Freud for concentrating on the emotional disorders of the individual. The central psychological problem of the twentieth century, Canetti argued, was not the individual. It was the new degenerative disease of the body politic: the mass movement. No one had studied the psychodynamics of the mass, could explain its behavior, or cure it. Yet, Canetti predicted, mass movements would dominate the rest of the century. It was hardly fair to criticize Freud for trying to cure what he thought he could cure. But Canetti had a point. The mass movement has become the dominant political phenomenon of the century. And it is brand new.

Most people still do not know what Canetti was talking about. When they hear the word "mass," they think of huge numbers of people streaming in all directions without purpose, without leadership, without commitment. But the mass of modern politics is akin to the critical mass of the atomic physicist. It is the minimum amount needed to bring about that maximum change, what the physicist calls a "change of state." To vary the metaphor, the mass of modern politics is akin to the massive cancer that overwhelms the human body even though it weighs only a pound.

The mass movement of modern politics is a small minority—no more than 5, at most 10 percent of the electorate. It dominates because it is organized, active, directed, and completely committed to a single cause. By contrast, the body politic, though large, is disorganized, inert, splintered, and not committed to anything. For the mass movement, its own political cause has absolute priority. For the rest of us, politics—and public affairs altogether—are at best one interest and rarely a major one. It is this mass movement, in the form of the "single-cause" pressure group, that increasingly paralyzes and tyrannizes political life in the developed countries.

Canetti wrote when Hitler was coming to power. He himself had first become aware of the mass movement as a schoolboy in Germany watching very small but highly organized semi-military groups attempt to grab power—the Communists in Munich in 1919, the Nazis four years later. Both attempts had failed. But by the time Canetti wrote, other such mass movements of tiny but totally organized single-cause gangs had already succeeded—Vladimir Ilich Lenin in Russia, Benito Mussolini in Italy.

The mass movement is not Lenin's invention; it is not even European in its origin. It was "Made in America." Its inventors were the two earliest American press barons, Joseph

Pulitzer and William Randolph Hearst. They first saw that the mass-circulation paper can be used—or misused—to create a tiny but highly vocal and disciplined pressure group. The two publishers pushed the United States into war with Spain in 1898. Politicians, almost without exception, were opposed to the war, and so was most of the population. But Pulitzer and Hearst made going to war with Spain the single issue around which they organized their readers. They instructed their readers to support any candidate, whatever else he stood for, as long as he voted for going to war with Spain, and to oppose any candidate, whatever else he stood for, unless he voted for war with Spain. The 5 or 8 percent of the vote that Pulitzer and Hearst mobilized was enough to get pro-war candidates elected and to defeat candidates who said maybe, let alone no.

For European "progressives" in the 1890s Spain was an "anachronism," "reactionary," and an enemy. America's going to war against Spain was thus hailed as a great "left" victory. The European left was then in dire need of victories. It had just come to realize that it had to give up the Marxist Utopia to gain majority support. Two of the leaders of Europe's militant left therefore seized upon Pulitzer and Hearst's invention to create similar small, single-cause mass movements of true believers in the Revolution.

The first was a Frenchman, Georges Sorel, who began to preach around 1905 that a general strike called by a very small but totally disciplined band of "proletarians" could overturn the "bourgeoisie" and destroy "capitalism." Revolution through general strike was actually tried three times in the twenties, first in Italy, in 1921, then in Great Britain in 1923, finally in Japan in 1926. It failed in Great Britain. But in both Italy and Japan the strike did overturn the existing order; the winners, however, were not the proletarians but Mussolini's Fascists in Italy and the military Fascists in the Japanese Army.

The second leftist disciple of the mass movement in Europe—and the most successful one—was Lenin. He founded his Bolshevik Party as a small minority of totally disciplined "true believers" who would not even attempt to attract mass support, would not make any compromise whatever, and would have only one single cause: power. Lenin had three successful disciples. One, another militant, Adolf Hitler in his book *Mein Kamp*—written in 1925–27— candidly acknowledged his indebtedness to Lenin. Mao Zedong ten years later adapted Lenin's mass movement to China. And in Italy, during World War I, the German sociologist Robert Michels adapted for use by a friend and disciple named Benito Mussolini what Lenin had invented earlier.

In the United States too the significance of Pulitzer and Hearst's invention was soon understood, not by the "revolutionary left" but by the Temperance movement. The prohibitionists in the United States had been trying for decades with practically no success to gain majority support for banning, or at least controlling, alcoholic beverages. After Pulitzer and Hearst they changed their strategy, and organized small, disciplined minorities that would gain power by supporting or opposing political candidates according to their stand on the single issue of Prohibition. Prohibition may actually have lost popular support in the first two decades of this century—its peak popularity probably occurred around 1870 or 1880. But by adopting the strategy of the mass movement, the prohibitionists forced the U.S. Congress to bar alcohol in 1919.

Single-cause pressure groups modeled on the Temperance movement have since come to dominate politics, especially in the United States. They may be concerned with the environment. They may be pro-abortionist or anti-abortionist. They may define the mission of America as high subsidies for a few thousand tobacco farmers in North Carolina. Whatever the single cause, the strategies of single-cause movements are always the same. They know no compromise. They hold their own single cause to be a moral absolute. They do not aim at gaining majority support or even at attracting majority following, otherwise they might have to compromise. And the slightest hint of any willingness to do so destroys their power. The single-cause mass movement does not trade votes. That its cause does not enjoy wide popular support is of no concern to the single-cause pressure group—something neither politicians nor journalists understand as a rule. Polls showing that the great majority of Americans are in favor of gun control or do not support subsidies to tobacco growers are irrelevant. The candidate who promises to support their cause gets their vote; the candidate who either does not promise to do so or hedges is being opposed. Nothing else counts.

An organized single-cause minority that can marshal 3 to 5 percent of the vote can rarely provide the margin of victory. Its opposition though often ensures defeat. It thus is rarely a force for positive action, but it succeeds in blocking whatever action it does not approve. Unlike the totalitarians, the single-cause group does not attempt to seize power. It does not even perceive itself as political, but as moral. The totalitarians were predators; the new mass movements are parasites. The totalitarians killed. The single-cause pressure group paralyzes.

The new mass movements are most visible and most powerful in the United States. But Europe has become infected. There are the "Greens" in Germany and Scandinavia. The "militants" of the left in Britain number no more than a few percent of the electorate, yet their single-cause positions—especially on unilateral nuclear disarmament—have for years now paralyzed the British Labour Party and guaranteed its defeat in election after election. In France the "Le Pen Nationalists" with their single cause of throwing out immigrants and foreigners have already succeeded in paralyzing the French center parties and may succeed in paralyzing the

French left as well. These small minorities all have the same strategy: commitment by a small, disciplined "mass" to a single cause as a moral absolute.

Single-cause, special-interest groups are highly powerful in Japan, more powerful even than in the United States. What the North Carolina tobacco farmers are to American politics, highly subsidized rice growers are to the politics of Japan. And there are good reasons to believe that such groups are equally plentiful and powerful in both Communist Russia and Communist China.

Because of these new mass movements, the locus of decision making in the political process is rapidly shifting from politicians and civil servants to lobbyists. In Roosevelt's America, the political bosses in the big cities provided the integrating force. So did local or regional politicians in the parliamentary countries of Western Europe and the heads of political factions in Japan. In all developed countries, the civil service is supposed to both support and counterbalance the politicians. Increasingly, however, policy making becomes special-interest manipulation, which can only be done by people who themselves have no political power base, no political agenda, in fact, no political mandate of any kind. Thus, policy will more and more be made behind the scenes and increasingly by threat or bribe. And, as a result, political decisions and actions increasingly have to be postponed until there is a "crisis," an "emergency," a "catastrophe." Only under such a threat does the single-cause, special-interest group lose its veto power.

No one yet knows an antidote to the political disease of single-interest pluralism. There may be ways to assuage it. One treatment—it would be quite effective in the United States—would be a change in the tax system so that there are no tax exemptions, no tax breaks, no tax deferments of any kind. Everybody pays tax at exactly the same rate on all incomes above a minimum level. (There might be three rates:

zero for incomes in the lowest 25 percent of the population; perhaps 15 percent for taxpayers with incomes between 25 and 75 percent; and 25 percent for the top 25 percent income earners.) Not all single-cause special interests are concerned with tax preferences, but a good many are. And a flat-rate tax system is desirable in itself. It would produce more revenue than any of the present complicated systems with their loopholes and special preferences, and would be easier and cheaper to run.

Another way to reduce the power of the single-cause special interests—it would have considerable impact in the United States, Japan, and West Germany—would be a change in financing campaigns for political office. Campaign contributions of any kind or from any source could be strictly prohibited. So would campaign expenses above a low level. Both winning and losing candidates (or parties) would then be reimbursed after the election on the basis of the votes they actually received. Such a change has often been proposed. So far politicians have shown remarkably little enthusiasm for it.

Even if such changes did come about, they would only assuage the monstrous tyranny of the small minority that affects the political system and paralyzes the political process. Can the disease be cured? Probably only when we have finally developed new political integrators to take the place of both the belief in salvation by society and in integration through the "economic estates of the realm." To find and develop such integrators will thus be one of the major demands on political leadership.

8

"BEWARE CHARISMA":
THE CHANGED DEMANDS ON
POLITICAL LEADERSHIP

As I am editing this chapter, George Bush is being sworn in in Washington as President of the United States. The campaign in which he gained office was unbearably dull, but the United States has had dull campaigns before. What distinguished the 1988 campaign was its ineffable blandness: to discuss an issue—any issue—would have alienated either party's most loyal, most committed, most zealous supporters. The Democratic candidate would have lost the support of liberals and progressives, had he addressed issues. The Republican candidate would equally have lost the conservatives. There was no program either candidate could have offered that would not have split his voting base into feuding splinters.

It is not only in America that political leaders have become bland, eschew issues and programs, and commit themselves as little as possible. Margaret Thatcher, the British prime minister—the most senior and the most successful political leader in today's free world—in her ten years on the job has concentrated on only three tasks: breaking the labor unions' stranglehold; privatization in industry, in housing, in education; and making sure that growing involvement in the European Economic Community does not endanger Britain's "special relationship" with the United States. On everything else she has been pragmatic, situation-focused, uncommitted.

Francois Mitterand, who has survived as president of France since 1981, came into office with an ambitious program: to create the France of the "Socialist Dream." Within five months—as already mentioned—he had to abandon the dream. Since then he has had only two policies: to stay in office and to put his supporters into key posts in government and business.

Another political survivor, Dr. Helmut Kohl, the West German chancellor, has no policy either, nor any program. He takes problems as they come. Should a Social Democrat replace Dr. Kohl in a future German election, there will almost certainly be a change in style only rather than one in substance.

Nor is Japan different. Twenty years ago, Japan had a prime minister who came to power with a most ambitious program: "to double within ten years Japan's GNP." The present prime minister, Noboru Takeshita, was elected (as a well-informed Japanese friend puts it), "because of his quiet competence in earlier government jobs, because he never committed himself, and because he made no waves."

The American media explained the blandness of the 1988 election campaign with the personalities of the contenders, and especially with their lack of "charisma." But general phenomena can never be explained by, or attributed to, local causes or specific personalities. They are generic and have generic causes. America's 1988 presidential candidates fought a bland campaign—without issues, without programs, without promises—precisely because none of the traditional issues, programs, or promises fit the political realities. Nor do any of the traditional alignments. But nothing else is available except traditional policies, promises, and alignments. This forces politics and politicians to be "dull," that is, pragmatic, task-focused rather than issue-focused, and above all, concerned far more with what might *repel* potential voters and constituents than with what might attract them. The press, the intellectuals, the political commentators want traditional politics, with their excitement, their sharp clashes, their clear-cut choices. The politicians know better—and they get elected. But they also know (as the prime minister in a mid-Victorian novel by Anthony Trollope put it) that "Government must go on." Hence the emphasis on competence, on not making waves, on getting things done, the emphasis on specific tasks and ad hoc solutions.

The public is right in its distrust of traditional leaders. They could only be demagogues—or failures, as Mitterand in France almost became. Traditional policies and programs, traditional alignments, traditional positions cannot accomplish anything. There is no place any more for political "Revolutions," for "New Deals," or "Fair Deals," or "New Societies." They do not even work as campaign slogans. Nor do the ideologies of salvation by society or the organization of power around interest blocs fit either the tasks to be done or the constituencies. Neither can support leadership. They can result only in misleadership.

The political motto for the new political realities has to be "Beware Charisma!" Charisma is "hot" today. There is an enormous amount of talk about it, and an enormous number of books written on the charismatic leader. There is nostalgia for the time when politics was exciting and glamorous. But the desire for charisma is a political death wish. No century has seen more leaders with more charisma than our twentieth century, and never have political leaders done greater damage than the four giant charismatic leaders of this century—Stalin, Mussolini, Hitler, and Mao. What matters is not charisma. What matters is whether the leader leads in the right direction or misleads. And under present conditions charismatic leadership could not be anything but misleadership. It would lead toward yesterday rather than toward the new realities.

The charismatic leader, as this century shows, is always endangered. Like King Canute, he cannot command the tides. Reality is beyond his control. When he finds out that reality is the master, the charismatic leader becomes paranoid. Every one of the great charismatic leaders of this century ended up a maniac. He destroyed everything and finally himself—in Stalin's purges; in Hitler's "final solution"; in Mao's "Cultural Revolution." And Napoleon too was no longer sane when, already defeated in 1813 and 1814, he turned down half a dozen offers that would have kept him emperor of France within the country's historical borders, and instead insisted on remaining the master of Europe. Reality, is, however, always the master. It will not subordinate itself to the promises, the programs, the ideologies of the charismatic leader.

Charisma creates arrogance. The most charismatic American military leader was surely General Douglas MacArthur, and arguably the ablest one as well. Yet in the end his charisma made him so arrogant that he brushed aside orders from President Truman, his commander in chief, disregarded all the warnings of a Chinese counterattack in Korea, and blundered into disastrous—and totally unnecessary—military defeat.

Charisma without a program is always ineffectual. But there are no programs today. The worshippers of charismatic leadership in the United States always hark back to John F. Kennedy. But what did the Kennedy administration actually accomplish? Nothing at all in domestic politics. Internationally it caved in to the Communists over the Berlin Wall and invaded Cuba in the frivolous fiasco of the Bay of Pigs—which then invited the Russians to try their own Cuban adventure, thus bringing the world to the brink of World War III. Neither charisma with political substance nor charisma without it are what is needed. Unspectacular, undramatic, dull as they are, competent leaders, who don't make commitments and don't make waves, are vastly preferable.

The constructive achievements of this century were the work of completely uncharismatic people. The two military men who guided the Allies to victory in World War II—both Americans—were Dwight Eisenhower and George Marshall. Both were highly disciplined, highly competent, and deadly dull. That the non-Communist world recovered from Hitler and World War II—and in record time—we owe primarily to two men: Konrad Adenauer, the first chancellor of postwar Germany, and Harry Truman, the first American postwar President. Adenauer restored German society after twelve years of Nazi horror and total defeat. He largely invented the Europe into which he then integrated the outcast, post-Nazi Germany. Yet Adenauer was a gray, colorless, pedantic bureaucrat, and the perfect organization man. The British kicked him out as politically incompetent when, after Hitler's fall, he tried to go back to his pre-Nazi job as mayor of Cologne. If Hollywood had hired him, it would have been as an *Oberbuchhalter,* an accounting supervisor. What he had instead of charisma was vision, deep religious faith, a sense of duty, and a willingness to work very hard.

Harry Truman, the "accidental President," had even less charisma than Adenauer. Hollywood would have cast him as manager of a men's clothing store, which he was before he got a minor political patronage job when the store went bankrupt. Yet Truman saved postwar Europe from collapse into anarchy, communism, and despair. Again, all he had was moral seriousness, a deep sense of duty, a willingness to get the best advice and to work very hard.

And yet there are tremendous political tasks ahead. There is the urgent task of reversing the arms race to free the world from the increasingly counterproductive burden of arms spending. There is the common interest to save the environment from increasing pollution from which no one country benefits and all ultimately suffer. There are going to be horrendous foreign policy decisions and dilemmas as the Russian Empire decays. There is the need to think through the limits and function of government in a pluralist society and in a polity beset by the single-cause special interests. There is need for political leadership of the "new majority," the knowledge workers of the post-business society.

In these new tasks, the enemy is not *somebody else*. The enemy is *us*. Traditional political slogans, traditional political constituencies, traditional politics cannot handle these challenges. There are a few encouraging precedents, where new approaches, unimaginable only twenty-five years ago, have produced results. Only a decade ago pollution had almost killed the Mediterranean. It has been halted through joint action by the three industrial countries of its littoral: Spain, France, and Italy. Then there is President Reagan's success—totally unexpected even by him—in using the "hawks" of his own party and their desire for a tremendous increase in American military might to bring about the first real cutback in world armaments in the Intermediate Nuclear Missiles Treaty with the Soviet Union of 1988. Perhaps the greatest cause for hope for optimism is the fact that to the new majority, the knowledge workers, the old politics make no sense at all. But proven competence does.

None of the new political tasks is ideological. Nor are these interest issues. Most are not even national issues. And few, if any, could be dealt with as adversarial issues; few, if any, could thus be tackled as traditional political issues. Most of the decisions we face are over means. That the arms race threatens all of us, very few doubt any more. Nor is there much doubt of the need to slow down and control environmental pollution, or of the need to constrain the political pollution of the single-cause special interests. Traditional politics differed over ends. The new realities largely impose the ends. The question they raise is: What are the means of getting there?

Traditional political leadership organized around issues, that is, around disagreements over ends. Increasingly the task of the new political leadership will be to organize around agreement over ends, indeed, to mobilize the consensus on ends. And this also may be the only way to undercut the paralyzing power of the small minorities. The political leaders around now, the Thatchers, Mitterands, Kohls, Takeshitas, Bushes, the gray, workaholic experts, may be neither accident nor passing phase. We need serious commitment, willingness to concentrate on one or two priorities, terribly hard work, and competence.

But is this going to be enough? President Reagan at his first arms limitation meeting with Mr. Gorbachev in 1986 announced as his goal the abolition of all nuclear weapons by the year 2000. Universally ridiculed, he immediately backtracked. Should he have held fast to his vision? We don't need "charisma" or "programs." But we do need clear goals. We do need vision.

PART III

ECONOMY, ECOLOGY,
AND ECONOMICS

9

TRANSNATIONAL ECONOMY—
TRANSNATIONAL ECOLOGY

Everybody talks about the "world economy." It is indeed a new reality. But it is quite different from what most people—businessmen, economists, politicians—mean by the term. Here are some of the world economy's main features, its main challenges, its main opportunities:

• In the early or mid-seventies—with OPEC and with President Nixon's "floating" of the dollar—the world economy changed from being international to transnational. The transnational economy has now become dominant, controlling in large measure the domestic economies of the national states.

• The transnational economy is shaped mainly by money flows rather than by trade in goods and services. These money flows have their own dynamics. The monetary and fiscal policies of sovereign national governments increasingly react to events in the transnational money and capital markets rather than actively shaping them.

• In the transnational economy the traditional "factors of production," land and labor, increasingly become secondary.

Money, too, having become transnational and universally obtainable, is no longer a factor of production that can give one country a competitive advantage in the world market. Foreign-exchange rates matter only over short periods. Management has emerged as the decisive factor of production. It is management on which competitive position has to be based.

• In the transnational economy the goal is not "profit maximization." It is "market maximization." And trade increasingly follows investment. Indeed, trade is becoming a function of investment.

• Economic theory still assumes that the sovereign national state is the sole, or at least the predominant unit, and the only one capable of effective economic policy. But in the transnational economy there are actually *four* such units. They are what the mathematician calls "partially dependent variables," linked and interdependent but not controlled by each other. The national state is one of these units; individual countries—especially the major, developed, non-Communist ones—matter, of course. But increasingly decision-making power is shifting to a second unit, the region—the European Economic Community; North America; tomorrow perhaps a Far Eastern region grouped around Japan. Third, there is a genuine and almost autonomous world economy of money, credit, and investment flows. It is organized by information that no longer knows national boundaries. Finally, there is the transnational enterprise—not necessarily a big business, by the way—which views the entire developed non-Communist world as one market, indeed, as one "location," both to produce and to sell goods and services.

• Economic policy implies increasingly neither "free trade" nor "protectionism," but "reciprocity" between regions.

• There is an even newer transnational ecology. The environment no more knows national boundaries than does money or information. The crucial environmental needs—the protection of the atmosphere, for instance, and of the world's forests—cannot be met by national action or national law. They cannot be addressed as adversarial issues. They require common transnational policies, transnationally enforced.

• Finally: while the transnational world economy is reality, it still lacks the institutions it needs. Above all it needs transnational law.

The American Experience . . .

Because the United States is still the world's dominant economy—more than twice that of Japan—the American experience of the last two decades best illustrates the shift to the new economic realities. Everybody knows that in the early and mid-eighties American manufacturing industry all but collapsed. But, as so often happens, "everybody" is wrong. The reality is far more complicated. The overvalued dollar did create a tremendous American market for industrial imports during that period. American industrial exports did not however "collapse"; they grew in every year but one of the period. Within a year and a half after the dollar's overvaluation had been corrected in the fall of 1985, American manufacturing exports began to boom, even though Latin America, traditionally the best market for American manufactured goods, was still in deep crisis and not buying.

But also the same industries that were in trouble in the United States in the eighties—automobiles, steel, consumer electronics—soon found themselves in similar trouble in Western Europe as well. By the end of the decade the Europeans, despite heavy protection, were under greater pressure from Japanese and Korean imports than the Americans had ever been. The U.S. subsidiaries of Philips, the largest non-Japanese producer of consumer electronics, are doing well against Japanese and Korean competition. But the parent company in Europe—with plants in Holland, Germany, Britain, France, Austria, Italy, and Spain—is reeling under the onslaught from the Far East. Philips products have largely been pushed off the shelves in Great Britain by Korean imports, for instance. Ford has steadily increased its share of the U.S. market despite Japanese competition. Fiat and Renault, however, would have a hard time to compete against Toyota and Honda were Italy and France to open themselves to imports from Japan. Surely what is a worldwide upheaval in traditional manufacturing should not be blamed on purely American causes or events.

During the eighties American industrial companies also maintained their full share of the world markets—and even increased it. Goods made by American-domiciled companies and carrying American brand names accounted for some 20 percent of the sales of all manufactured goods worldwide both in 1980 and in 1988. In absolute figures, holding on to this share represents rapid growth, both in production and sales. For total sales of manufactured goods worldwide grew by half—or more—during that period. At the same time, American manufacturing companies considerably strengthened their control over, and their revenues from, the goods sold under their brand names overseas. At the beginning of the eighties most American-branded goods sold in Japan (the world's second-largest market and the second-largest market also for a great many American brands) were produced by joint ventures in which the Japanese partner owned a majority. By the end of the eighties most of these joint ventures had passed under American ownership—either 100 percent or majority—as Americans used the high-value dollar to buy out their Japanese partners.

All told it was not a "collapse of manufacturing" that underlay the enormous U.S. trade deficit of the eighties; it was the worldwide collapse of commodity prices and commodity exports. Beginning in 1981, world market prices for farm products and industrial raw materials collapsed. And so did purchases of both. Raw material prices as measured against the prices of manufactured goods fell in the eighties to the lowest levels ever recorded, lower even than during the Great Depression of the thirties. By the end of the eighties there were only two major markets for foodstuffs left: Japan and the Soviet Union. Even India, plagued for centuries by endemic famine, had become an exporter of farm products, and China was reaching self-sufficiency in food.

The United States historically has been the world's largest exporter of farm products and of raw materials altogether. Indeed, it has been the only major developed country (other than Canada) that was integrated into the world economy through raw material exports rather than through exports of manufactured goods. Had U.S. raw material exports remained, in volume and in price, at the relative levels of 1978, U.S. trade deficits in the eighties would have been a full third smaller. Another third was accounted for by the impact of the prolonged raw material slump on America's traditional customers for manufactured goods, the raw material-producing countries of Latin America. And of the rest of the U.S. trade deficit of the eighties, most represents rapidly rising petroleum imports rather than shortfalls in manufacturing.

In terms of the productivity and competitiveness of U.S. agriculture, the dollar was not "overvalued" at 250 yen to the dollar. It may even have been undervalued. What made the dollar appear overvalued was the world market slump in raw material and food prices rather than anything happening in or to U.S. manufacturing industry.

The developments following the downward adjustment of the dollar against the yen that started in the fall of 1985 are equally at odds with what everybody "knew" would happen.

Instead of a "minor" adjustment of foreign-exchange values—a yen/dollar ratio of 225 or 210 was generally expected—the dollar went into "free fall," losing half its value in yen within fifteen months. But raw material prices—always the first ones to adjust to foreign-exchange fluctuations—did not respond at all this time. Instead, they actually continued their decline in U.S. dollars. As a result American prices and wages did not rise at all as U.S. living costs remained stable and even declined slightly. This then meant a very sharp drop in food and raw material costs for everyone but the Americans. By the fall of 1988, for instance, the Japanese actually paid in yen no more than a third of what they had paid three years earlier for their food and their industrial raw materials—primarily because of the 50 percent fall of the dollar and secondarily because *in dollars* food and raw material prices were still going down, quite substantially. Despite their lower prices, however, American exports of agricultural products and industrial raw materials did not increase, nor did those of the other food and raw material exporters such as Brazil.

A sharp devaluation of a currency *must*—according to all theory and all experience—sharply increase a country's exports and sharply decrease a country's imports. U.S. exports did rise, and sharply, though not until a year and a half after the dollar's devaluation. By the end of 1988 the rise in exports of U.S. manufactured goods had narrowed the trade deficit by the one third that can be considered to have been caused, in the first place, by the earlier dollar overvaluation. But industrial imports into the United States—which according to all theory and all earlier experience should have all but disappeared—kept on increasing!

Equally unprecedented is the behavior of money and investment flows. The United States is the first major debtor in financial history to owe all its foreign debt in its own currency. The devaluation of the dollar by 50 percent against the currencies of America's main creditors, Japan and West Germany (the two countries with the biggest export surpluses in their trade with the U.S.), thus effectively cut in half the value of their enormous dollar holdings. Yet they—and all the other U.S. creditors—kept pumping money into the United States and supporting the U.S. government deficit by buying U.S. government obligations.

Finally, America's creditors—the British and Canadians first, then the West Germans, and last the Japanese—began to convert their financial dollar claims into investments by buying American businesses and American real estate, made "cheap" by a devalued dollar. This, of course, is exactly what economic theory predicted they would do and, in fact, would have to do. Still, their investments—especially those made by the Japanese—got tremendous publicity.

But no one noticed—in large part because it contradicted everything that economic theory would consider "economically rational" behavior—that American companies invested during this period considerably *more* abroad than foreigners invested in the United States. In 1987, for instance, all foreigners, with the British in the lead, invested some $35 billion in American businesses and American real estate. In the same year American companies invested at least $50 billion in their subsidiaries and affiliates abroad, especially in the European Common Market. As a result American investments in businesses abroad amounted to some $310 billion by the end of 1987, topping foreign direct investments in the United States by a comfortable margin. If the Americans had behaved rationally, that is, according to economic theory, they would have *sold* $50 billion worth of foreign investments to maximize their profits. Instead, they sacrificed immediate profit to maximize market standing, precisely as the foreigners—Japanese, Germans, British—had been doing when they maintained and even increased their sales to the United States, even though the dollars they got were worth so much less in their own currencies.

. . . And Its Lessons

The first lesson of the American experience is that the raw material economy and the industrial economy have become "uncoupled." For the developed non-Communist countries, the raw material economy has become marginal.

If there was one thing proven in business cycle theory it was that a sharp and prolonged slump in food and raw material prices will always be followed within eighteen months by a serious and prolonged crisis in the industrial economy. This was true in the eighteenth and nineteenth centuries. It still held for the recessions of 1907 and 1921 and for the Great Depression of 1929. By 1989 the raw material economy worldwide had been in its most serious and most prolonged depression ever for almost a decade. Yet the industrial economies were booming.

It was similarly well-proven theory that raw material prices respond immediately to foreign-exchange fluctuations. When the international value of the dollar went down, the dollar prices of raw materials should have risen by a corresponding percentage. Instead, they kept on falling. One explanation is the worldwide surplus of farm products caused by the tremendous expansion of agricultural production, especially in the developed non-Communist countries. At the same time farm population in all non-Communist developed countries has shrunk to where it is almost insignificant statistically. A sharp drop in farm income and purchasing power (in the U.S. farm incomes dropped by two thirds in some regions between 1984 and 1987) has little effect on national income, national purchasing power, and consumer buying.

Equally important: the economy is steadily becoming less material-intensive. Some 60 percent of the costs of the representative industrial product of the 1920s, the automobile, lay in raw materials and energy. The raw material and energy costs of the representative industrial product of the 1980s, the semiconductor microchip, are less than 2 percent. Copper wire with a raw material and energy content of close to 80 percent is rapidly being replaced in telephone cables by glass fiber with a raw material and energy content of 10 percent.

Japan increased its industrial production between 1965 and 1985 two and a half times, barely increasing its raw material and energy consumption at all. The nation's manufactured products contained in 1985 less than half as much material and energy as they had contained twenty years earlier. The newest "energy" of all—information—has no raw material or energy content at all. It is totally "knowledge-intensive."

Manufacturing is increasingly becoming uncoupled from labor. American manufacturing *production* during the 1980s steadily increased. Manufacturing employment dropped steadily to where in 1988 it took no more than two fifths of the man-hours of blue-collar labor it took in 1973 to manufacture the same volume of goods.

Where none of the traditional "factors of production"—land, labor, money—determine competitiveness or competitive advantage any longer, trade is increasingly being replaced by investment as the world economy's economic driver. Investment used to follow trade. Now trade follows investment. Proximity to, and "feel" for, the market become decisive. And that requires a base within the market; it requires market presence and market standing. It requires investment in production, in other words. "Sales" then become "return on the investment" in the market. If the investment is not maintained, there will be no sales. If the market grows or changes while the investment in it stays the same, there will similarly be no sales.

This explains why the Japanese and the West Germans chose to maintain the dollar price on their goods in the American market even though the dollar lost half its value in yen and marks. It explains why the Japanese build plants in Europe even though their costs are very high as European currencies have not gone down in relation to the Japanese yen. And it explains why American companies plow back the earnings of their foreign subsidiaries rather than take large immediate dollar profits. They all are maximizing their market standing.

Another lesson of the American experience during the eighties is that business has shifted from being multinational to being transnational.

Many of America's large companies in industries most affected by foreign imports were saved by the profits of their subsidiaries abroad in the years of the overvalued dollar. The Ford Motor Company, for instance. More important, Ford's subsequent turnaround and recovery in the U.S. market were based on products and processes developed in Europe and by Ford's Japanese affiliate, Mazda. Conversely Honda—a Japanese-domiciled automobile manufacturer—is trying to gain leadership in the Japanese automobile market where it has been a distant third, by shipping American-made Honda cars back to Japan.

The traditional multinational—invented in the middle years of the nineteenth century by U.S. and German industrialists—consists of a parent company with foreign "daughters." The parent company designs and manufactures for its domestic market. The daughters do not design at all. They produce locally whatever products the parent designs and sell those in their own markets.

The distinction between parent and daughter is increasingly blurring. In the transnational company, design is done anyplace within the system. Major pharmaceutical companies now have research laboratories in five or six countries, in the United States, Great Britain, Japan, Switzerland. They do their research wherever there are research scientists. They produce wherever the economics of manufacturing dictate—IBM produces personal computers for all of Europe in two locations and disk drives in one. A major pharmaceutical manufacturer makes and sells prescription drugs in 164 countries, but all fermentation work is done in one plant, in Ireland. The treasurer in the transnational company centrally manages money for all the members of the group rather than have the U.K. company manage money in London, the West German company manage money out of Frankfurt, the U.S. company manage money in New York, and so on. And the top management of the transnational—even if all executives are still located in the same country—is not the top management of the parent. Each unit including the parent company has its own, local management. Top management is transnational, and so are the company's business plans, business strategies, and business decisions.

Most people think of giant companies when they hear the word "transnational." But increasingly middle-sized and even small businesses operate in the world economy rather than in one or two countries. It is actually easier for the middle-sized and even for the small company to operate without much regard for national boundaries. Unlike large companies they are politically barely visible.

The American experience shows also that to have leadership in any area in the non-Communist developed world, a business—in manufacturing, in finance, in services—has to have a strong, if not a leadership, position in all areas of the "Triad" of North America, Western Europe, and Japan. The three do not constitute one market, but they do constitute one economy. Any firm in any of the three areas potentially competes with any firm in the other two. Thirty years ago most automobile manufacturers were content with leadership in their own domestic market. Fiat, for instance, did not aggressively sell outside of Italy. The other Europeans did not aggressively sell in Italy. Now Fiat is trying to become a "European" leader. And so are the Japanese.

The General Electric Company (GE) has long been the unchallenged leader in a large number of markets in the United States. In the 1980s management decided to get out of all areas anywhere, including the United States—even

125

profitable ones—in which it could not attain a major position worldwide. Instead, it expanded where it could obtain worldwide market leadership. It sold off a number of divisions, including small appliances and semiconductor microchips, which were profitable market leaders in the U.S. but offered no opportunities internationally. At the same time GE acquired a number of businesses abroad, especially in Europe— medical electronics, for instance—where management saw opportunity to become a leader. A number of large European and Japanese companies are conducting a similar strategy: Imperial Chemicals of Great Britain, Hoechst, the German chemical giant, and Japan's Sony. So do quite a few middle-sized and even small manufacturers, but increasingly also banks, insurance firms, even building-maintenance companies and contractors. "Any business I can reach by telephone is a potential customer as well as a potential competitor," as the chief executive officer of a medium-sized, low-tech company in the United States puts it.

A hundred years ago the Germans had to learn to manage even a strictly local firm—say a cigar maker in Hamburg—as a national business. Otherwise a cigar maker from Munich or Stuttgart would take away their local market. Fifty years ago every American firm—say an adhesives company in Massachusetts supplying local offices and banks—had to learn to manage itself as a continental business. Otherwise an adhesives manufacturer from southern California would suddenly appear and take over its "regional" market. At present even the small sausage maker in Belgium has to learn to run his firm as a "European" business. Otherwise a sausage maker from Spain will take over his national market. Increasingly, firms will have to learn to see themselves as transnational businesses. Otherwise a Japanese, a Korean, a German, a Canadian or an American will push them out of their own home market.

Symbol Economy versus Real Economy

One final and important lesson: the transnational economy is shaped and driven by money flows. These money flows have their own dynamics, which do not necessarily fit traditional economic rationality.

The big question is not what made the dollar go down in 1985. The question is what held it up so long. From 1971, when President Nixon "floated" the dollar, its foreign-exchange value was supposed to adjust to the ups and downs of the U.S. trade balance. From 1982 on, the United States had fast-mounting trade deficits, which soon exceeded anything ever seen before. Yet the dollar stubbornly stayed up at what everyone soon knew was an "unrealistically high" exchange rate. Then, when it fell, it went down to an exchange rate that was equally "unrealistically low" considering relative costs and productivities.

The only explanation for the dollar's behavior is that the "real" economy of goods and services no longer dominates the transnational economy; the symbol economy of money and credit does. Every day the London Interbank market turns over ten to fifteen times the amount of transnational currencies such as Eurodollars, Euromarks, or Euroyen needed to finance world trade in goods and services. The amounts traded on the major foreign-exchange markets— New York, London, Tokyo, Singapore, Zurich, Frankfurt— are many times what world industry and world commerce require. Ninety percent or more of the transnational economy's financial transactions do not serve what economists would consider an economic function. They serve purely financial functions. These money flows have their own rationality, of course. But they are in large part political rationalities: anticipation of government decisions as to central bank interest rates or foreign-exchange rates, taxes, government deficits and government borrowings, or political-risk assessment.

127

Yet, as the American experience shows, it is the symbol economy that largely controls the real economy.

One implication of this is that every business will have to learn to manage its foreign-exchange exposure. Managers must now assume that foreign-exchange rates matter even if the company's business is purely domestic, or appears to be so. They will have to assume that foreign-exchange rates are politically determined and therefore inherently unstable. Finally, they will have to accept responsibility for protecting the business against foreign-exchange risks just as they are responsible for protecting the business against any other foreseeable risk. Foreign-exchange fluctuations have become an ordinary cost of doing business. This is the opposite of the assumption on which most businesses in the developed non-Communist countries are still being run: that foreign-exchange rates are—or at least should be—inherently stable. If foreign-exchange fluctuations occur, they are considered "acts of God." They are, in fact, acts of men and especially of governments. The timing of these fluctuations can often no more be predicted than that of many other events such as a fire or an embezzlement. But it can be predicted that they will occur, and frequently.

No More Superpower

Because of the emergence of the transnational company and of the symbol economy as the determinant force in the world market, there is no more economic superpower. No matter how big, powerful, and productive a country may be, it competes every day for its world market position. No one country can, in fact, expect long to maintain a competitive lead in technology, in management, in innovation, in design, in entrepreneurship; but it does not matter much to the transnational company which country is in the lead. It does business in all of them and is at home in all of them. However, the individual company too can no longer take its leadership position for granted. There is no more "superpower" in industry, either; there are only competitors. A company's home country becomes a "location," that is a headquarters and communications center. But in any one industry there are a number of companies—some American, some German, some British, some Japanese—which together are the "superpowers" in that industry worldwide. Managers need increasingly to base business policy on this new transnational structure of industry and markets.

Adversarial Trade and Reciprocity

The advent of the transnational company is a structural change in the world economy. So is the emergence of the new major economic power: Japan (and all of Southeast Asia in Japan's wake). And every structural change in a system changes the rules that govern it.

Trade in Adam Smith's eighteenth century was *complementary* trade. England sold wool to Portugal that Portugal could not produce, while Portugal sold wine to England that England could not produce. The English bought from India cotton that they could not grow, in exchange for machine-made cotton cloth that eighteenth-century India could not produce. The entry of the United States and Germany into the world economy in mid-nineteenth century brought about a shift to *competitive* trade. The Americans and the Germans both sold chemicals and electrical machinery in competition with one another and bought chemicals and electrical machinery from each other. Almost unknown in 1850, competitive trade had become dominant by 1900.

The emergence of new, non-Western trading countries—foremost the Japanese—creates what I would call *adversarial* trade.

Complementary trade seeks to establish a partnership. Competitive trade aims at creating a customer. Adversarial trade aims at dominating an industry. Complementary trade

129

is a courtship. Competitive trade is fighting a battle. Adversarial trade aims at winning the war by destroying the enemy's army and its capacity to fight.

When competitive trade first became important, the English cried "foul." They charged the new competitors, the Americans and the Germans, with conspiracy. Similarly the West now cries "foul" and charges the Japanese with conspiracy for engaging in adversarial trade. Both the competitive trade of a century ago and the adversarial trade of today reflect objective needs and circumstances far more than they reflect deliberate attempts to defeat or to destroy. The Japanese themselves did not at first understand what they had begun to practice. In the early 1960s, when they had just barely recovered from the destruction of World War II, they saw themselves—with good reason—as backward in technology and even more so in marketing competence. It was logical for them to protect their home market against competition from abroad, which in those years meant primarily the United States. It also made sense for the Japanese to concentrate exports on the few industries in which they could hope to be able to be competitive, industries where markets had been well developed, in which the technology was available, and in which the Japanese could obtain substantial sales by doing a little better what was already done well. These industries—automobiles, steel, consumer electronics, photography, and optics—still had high labor content in those days. Thus Japan's ability to use the new and powerful management technology, training, to make low-wage workers fully productive enabled them to be effective competitors in developed Western markets. At the same time they still felt so backward—and indeed were so for a long time—as to have to keep out foreign competition. And this then led step by step to adversarial trade, in which the aim is to gain market control by destroying the enemy, or to obtain such predominance in a market that it would be almost impossible for newcomers to challenge the market leader.

Still, adversarial trade changes the basic rules, and drastically. In the first place it can no longer be assumed that competition is entirely beneficial—the basic postulate of the economist. It was one of the very great triumphs of nineteenth-century economics to prove—against serious doubt—that competitive trade is ultimately beneficial to both partners. To be sure, the Swiss plant that is losing business to a French competitor may have to lay people off. But, economists argued, this loss of existing Swiss jobs would be outweighed by new Swiss jobs created because Swiss consumers had more purchasing power, bought more, and invested more. Adversarial trade, however, is unlikely to be beneficial to both sides. If the attacked manufacturer, for example, an American optical company, survives an attack by a Korean manufacturer, it will become more competitive. Then competition is indeed ultimately beneficial. The aim in adversarial trade, however, is to drive the competitor out of the market altogether rather than to let it survive. When the attacking country is still closed to imports—or at least severely restricts them—the competitor under attack cannot effectively counterattack. It cannot win; it will at best not lose everything.

Adversarial trade thus challenges the conventional assumptions. Clearly protectionism that shuts off one's economy is the wrong answer. It can only make one's own industry even less competitive. But free trade is not the answer, either. One answer is to form economic regions or blocs: the economic merger of the European Economic Community planned for 1992; the North American Free Trade Zone which the 1988 U.S.-Canada Free Trade Agreement is trying to create; or perhaps, in the future, a Japan-centered Pacific Rim region. This would give smaller economies the large region and market they need to create the "critical mass" of production and sales needed to be competitive.

Regionalism creates a unit capable of an effective trade policy that transcends both protectionism and free trade. It creates a unit capable of *reciprocity*. And reciprocity is clearly the only trade policy that can effectively work in a world economy that features adversarial trade. Free trade can work under reciprocity if the other side reciprocates. But there will be protectionism if that is what either side chooses.

So far the United States has had a bias in favor of free trade in most areas (significant exceptions are agriculture, defense, and transportation). Japanese banks for instance can do what no American bank can do: they can run a full banking business in every state of the Union. Yet no foreign bank can operate a full banking business anywhere in Japan. Similarly, Japanese or Korean contractors are awarded contracts for major public works in the United States—for example, building a new museum in Los Angeles—whereas public-works contracts in Japan have so far been given exclusively to Japanese firms. Under reciprocity, each country's business would enjoy the same degree of access to the other country's markets, and no more. Indeed, reciprocity is the only way to prevent the world economy from regressing into extreme protectionism.

Reciprocity is fast emerging as the new integrating principle of the world economy. It is clearly going to be the main trade policy of the European Economic Community (EEC), if only because it alone offers a compromise between the traditional protectionists in the EEC (the French and the Italians) and the traditional free traders (the British and the Germans). It is fast becoming also the policy that the United States is choosing for economic relations with Japan, with Korea, and with Brazil. Reciprocity is thus likely to become the vehicle for the integration of the world economy just as competitive trade was the vehicle for the integration of the international economy during the last one hundred and fifty years.

Unlike traditional free trade and traditional protectionism, reciprocity will not be confined to trade in goods. Services have already become as important as goods in the world economy and require reciprocity even more. The treatment of investments is just as important as trade. The world economy is increasingly being integrated and held together by investment rather than by trade alone. Yet the differences in the treatment of investment are even greater between individual countries than they are with respect to trade. In some countries, even highly developed ones such as France or Japan, decisions on investment—whether by nationals or by foreigners—are arbitrary and heavily political. Eventually, as discussed later in this chapter, we will have to develop a legal system for international investment. In the meantime, reciprocity alone can work.

Equally important will be reciprocity with respect to intellectual property, patents, technological trade-marks, copyrights, but also with respect to professional services.

The Transnational Ecology

The final new reality in the world economy is the emergence of the transnational ecology. Concern for the ecology, the endangered habitat of the human race, will increasingly have to be built into economic policy. And increasingly concern for the ecology and ecological policies will transcend national boundaries. The main dangers to the human habitat are increasingly global—and so will be the policies needed to protect and preserve it. We still talk of "environmental protection" as if it were protection of something that is outside of, and separate from, man. But what is endangered are the survival needs of the human race. Until the nineteenth century, the never-ending challenge was the protection of mankind and its habitat against the forces of nature: epidemics, predators, floods, hurricanes. These forces are still as powerful as ever. The recent eruption of AIDS, the new plague, should have stilled all the prattle about "the conquest of nature." But in this century a new need has arisen: to protect nature against man. Indeed, awareness of the problem hardly existed until after World War II. Since then the threat has grown explosively, and it has totally changed character.

Most people still see the problem as it originally moved into our field of vision, that is, as a series of local, isolated, specific events: the smog over Los Angeles or Mexico City, the extinction of this or that animal species, the oil spill on a beach. But, as has become abundantly clear, even purely local environmental events are not "local" in their consequences. We now know that pollution knows no boundaries. Sulfur emissions from steel mills in America's Midwest become acid rain blighting Canadian forests. Toxic effluents discharged into the Rhine by chemical plants in Switzerland or in France's Alsace poison Holland's drinking water. Radioactive particles from a nuclear accident in the Ukraine contaminate Sweden's vegetables and make undrinkable the milk of Scots cows.

It is still generally believed that the threat to environment and ecology is confined to the developed countries and is, indeed, a result of industrialization, of the automobile, of affluence. But the greatest ecological catastrophe-in-the-making—and the one most difficult to contain, let alone reverse—is the destruction of the world's tropical forests by the least advanced, least developed, poorest inhabitants of the earth: destitute peasants using primitive methods and age-old tools. And no one voices any longer the dogmatic assertion that "pollution" is a product of capitalism and cannot happen under socialism—an article of the Communist faith only a few years ago. The greatest ecological disaster so far is the near-destruction of the world's largest body of fresh water, Lake Baikal in Siberia; Beijing and Budapest are fully as polluted as Mexico City, and do as little to solve the problem.

The destruction of the ecology on which humankind's survival depends is thus a common task. To tackle it as a national task is futile—though obviously a good deal of national, and even local, implementation will be needed. It is futile too to try to tackle it adversarially, with one country accusing its neighbor of befouling the environment—the Dutch accusing the French, the Swedes accusing the British, the Canadians accusing the Americans. Inevitably the accused country will proclaim its innocence and deny that there is a problem. No effective action can be taken until we accept that serious environmental damage anywhere is everybody's problem and threatens all of us.

This will require a major change in the way we think about the economy. Economists have been wont to consider pollution and environmental damages as "externalities." The costs are borne by the entire community rather than by the activity itself. But this will no longer do for environmental damage. There is no incentive not to pollute. On the contrary, to pollute without paying for it confers a distinct competitive advantage on those who pollute the worst. To treat environmental impacts as "externalities" can also no longer be justified theoretically. During the last century every developed country has converted industrial accidents from an externality into a direct cost of doing business. Every developed country has adopted workmen's compensation under which the employer pays an insurance premium based on its own accident experience, which makes the damage done by unsafe operations a direct cost of doing business. Workmen's compensation assumes that industrial activity is inherently dangerous; accidents are thus bound to happen. This was bitterly fought at the time as a "license to kill" by reformers dedicated to making the workplace safe. Workmen's compensation has done more, however, to reduce the incidence of industrial accidents than safety regulations or factory inspection.

Making environmental threat or damage a direct cost of doing business—for example, by levying a heavy fee on traffic in or out of a city during the rush hours—would have substantial psychological effect. It would also spur work on finding

135

substitutes for ecologically unsafe substances or practices. Such substitutes might for instance cut sharply America's worst pollution, the runoff from toxic or non-degradable pesticides, herbicides, and fertilizers from the farms. Substances that do serious harm and cannot be replaced by harmless ones can be forbidden—the way fluorocarbons are in the process of being outlawed.

Environmental action has to be local. Cleaning up the most polluted oceans—the shallow inland seas like the Baltic, the Mediterranean, the Sea of Cortez—requires that the riparian states clean up the biggest polluters, the municipal sewers. But such action has to be based on a common, transnational commitment. Transnational agreements alone cannot halt, let alone reverse, the environmental destruction in and by the developing countries. Yet that is where the damage is greatest—simply because what threatens the ecology the most is population pressure rather than industry.

Protection of the environment today requires international ecological laws. The nineteenth century offers a precedent. When steamship and railroad began to make possible large-scale travel, contagious diseases formerly confined to the tropics—such as yellow fever and cholera—invaded the countries of the Temperate Zone and threatened to become pandemics. They were contained by quarantines that kept people out of infected areas. A century later, during the New Deal period of the thirties, the U.S. government abolished child labor despite stubborn opposition by a number of southern states, by forbidding the shipment across state lines of goods produced by under-age youngsters.

We might similarly "quarantine" polluters and forbid shipment in international commerce of goods produced under conditions that seriously pollute or damage the human habitat—e.g., by polluting the oceans, by raising the temperature of the atmosphere, or by depleting its ozone. This will be decried as "interference with sovereign nations"—and so it is. It will probably require that the developed rich countries compensate the developing poor ones for the high costs of environmental protection, such as sewage treatment plants. In fact, environmental protection might well be the most productive purpose of foreign aid and far more successful than the development aid of the last four decades. Major problems would still remain even then. Foremost among them is the rapid destruction of the tropical forests by the pressure of land-hungry subsistence farmers, which threatens permanently to make arid and infertile large areas, including parts of the Temperate Zone.

The nineteenth century cured two of mankind's oldest scourges, the slave trade and piracy on the high seas, by transnational action. It declared both to be common enemies of humanity, the suppression of which was in the interest of any country at any time. The threat to the human habitat, the ecology, is a recent threat. But it is a greater threat than the slave trade or piracy ever were, and a threat to everyone. If it can be averted at all, it can be averted only by transnational commitment and joint action.

Protecting the Transnational Economy

Just as important as the protection of the natural habitat against the inroads of economic activity is the protection—and regulation—of the new man-made economic habitat, the transnational economy. On it depend the jobs, the livelihood, and the standard of living of practically everyone in the non-Communist world, both in the developed and the developing countries. The economic realities of the transnational economy have emerged, at least in outline. We still, however, do not have the law that the new realities require. And we need the direct opposite of what is now in place.

If this century has taught one lesson, it is that of interdependence: no part of the developed world prospers unless all do. In particular, there is no prosperity for the victor in modern war unless the vanquished recovers. It is clear self-interest for every single participant in the world economy—or at least for every single developed country—to have all the others recover as fast as possible from the destruction and dislocation of warfare. Above all, it is to the self-interest of every single participant in the world economy to restore as fast as possible the economic ties war has cut, to restore transnational confidence, and to restore the transnational flow of goods and investments. This was understood and acted on by President Truman, and explains why World War II was followed by the biggest and longest economic expansion in history, whereas World War I led to history's longest and most severe economic contraction and crisis.

We therefore need international laws that, in wartime, protect the resources required to rebuild the peacetime economy. This was in fact what Europe had for several hundred years, from the middle of the seventeenth to the end of the nineteenth century. During these two hundred and fifty years civilians, their persons and their property, were considered non-combatants and under the special protection of warring governments. However fiercely fought, neither side in the American Civil War imprisoned non-combatant citizens of the other side or impounded their property. A few years later, in the Franco-Prussian War of 1870–71, the Germans besieged Paris and subjected it to heavy bombardment. Yet they permitted business correspondence to enter and leave the city; and neither the besieging Germans nor the besieged French imprisoned each other's civilians or confiscated their property.

This doctrine—that war is being waged against soldiers and not against civilians—was abandoned by the British during the Boer War of 1899–1902. The British then invented the concentration camp in which they imprisoned Boer women and children in order to force their fighting men into submission. And they confiscated the Boers' farms as "the property of enemies." At the time these were rightly considered barbarous innovations. But twelve years later, in World War I, the British converted these barbarous innovations into new legal principles. Since then, both the person and the property of civilian subjects of an enemy government are treated as enemies in wartime, allowed neither rights nor legal protection. Their person is imprisoned, their property confiscated.

These are the wrong principles and the wrong policies for a transnational economy. We now need international law that establishes it as the clear duty of governments to protect, to conserve, and to defend during wartime the person and the property of non-combatant civilians of enemy nationality as long as they refrain from hostile words and acts. We need international law that codifies the common interest that all countries in the transnational and interdependent economy have in restoring prosperity once the fighting stops.

One of the proudest achievements of the nineteenth century—and one of its enduring ones—was the International Red Cross which the Swiss Jean-Henri Dunant founded in 1864. It provided, for the first time in history, for the protection and humane treatment of enemy soldiers, whether wounded or taken prisoner. What we need now is international law that protects enemy civilians, their person and their property. Such law would protect every country's interest in the world economy and its ability to survive war and recover from it. It was not a Great Power but an unknown citizen of a small neutral country who devised the Red Cross and called on the military powers of his time to join it. It may require political leadership for new transnational laws to be instigated in peacetime. But whichever country leads, it is likely to be followed soon—the need is as obvious to every country as the need to protect fighting men and prisoners of war had become in the mid-nineteenth century. But the need is also just as urgent.

10

THE PARADOXES
OF ECONOMIC DEVELOPMENT

Few people these days could imagine the excitement and enthusiasm when President Harry Truman committed the United States to worldwide economic development in his 1950 Point Four speech. There was equal enthusiasm when ten years later President John F. Kennedy proclaimed the Alliance for Progress that was to pull Latin America out of poverty in a decade. President Kennedy's picture still hangs on the walls of peasant huts from Mexico to Patagonia. Economic development—a term that had not even been in common use earlier—became the great exciting "discovery." But, as "everyone knows," economic development has not worked. It is seen as a dismal failure. Actually no earlier period in economic history saw as much economic development—and as large in scale and scope—as the forty years since President Truman's Point Four. The key to this paradox is that the two sides—those who see failure and those who see success—look at two different things. One looks at what development was supposed to be—and that has indeed been a failure. The other sees the development that no one expected but that actually did happen.

There is a second paradox and a new reality: the most popular and seemingly most successful of the policies that did work no longer do so. One—exporting to developed countries the products of low-wage but highly productive labor—requires that manufacturing in the developed countries be labor-intensive. It no longer is. Another—its nineteenth-century name is "infant-industry protection"—became counterproductive just when it had become most effective. Today it has proven a root cause for the economic crises that now afflict the Third World countries that developed the fastest, such as Brazil and Mexico. It is grinding India's industrial development to a standstill. And it is also at the bottom of the growing economic tensions between Japan and the West.

The Successes

The Far East is, of course, the showpiece of successful development, experiencing both the fastest and the least expected growth. In 1950, Japan had barely begun to emerge from wartime devastation. Most Japanese then still doubted that their country would ever regain the prewar economic levels. And those levels were low enough: half of the Japanese population were still subsistence farmers in the thirties. Further, although Japan had built a strong arms industry in the decade before World War II—dismantled, of course, after the defeat—its civilian industry had a well-deserved reputation for poorly designed, low-quality products and for singularly vicious labor relations. Japan's standard of living and its productivity in 1937 were no more than a third that of depression-wracked America.

In 1952, when the Korean War ended, South Korea was even more devastated than Japan had been in 1945; the country had no industries at all and almost no trained and edu-

141

cated people. Hong Kong until the 1960s was a trading port without industries. Singapore was little more than a British naval base. And Taiwan had little except a few plantations that supplied the country's colonial masters, the Japanese, with high-cost sugar.

The northern rim of the Mediterranean was almost as poor and backward as the Far East. The sole industry was in the foothills of the Alps, at the very extreme of Italy. Some regions are still poor—Sicily and the "boot" of Italy, for instance. But Italy as a whole now boasts a higher income than Britain. Southern France has grown into a major industrial as well as a major agricultural region. And Spain and Portugal are developing even faster.

The American South—Georgia, the Carolinas, Alabama, Tennessee, Louisiana, Mississippi—was dirt-poor at the end of World War II. There is still poverty there, just as there is in Korea or in Spain—backcountry Mississippi, for instance. But as a whole the South is now only a shade behind the rest of the affluent United States.

Then there are the rapidly industrializing countries of Latin America. Brazil has become the world's eighth-largest industrial power. In 1950 it was still agricultural, an exporter of coffee and cocoa, not even on the world's industrial map. Now it is a major industrial exporter of footwear, of war materiel such as tanks and airplanes, of machine tools. Mexico too has moved from being agricultural in 1950 to being heavily industrialized, with an industrial output equal to that of the Iberian Peninsula.

When the British left, India had almost no middle class. Forty years later, India has a well-educated middle class of 100 million people out of a total of 800 million. They have middle-class standards of living, middle-class competence, and middle-class expectations. And India, plagued by recurrent famines for two hundred years, has become self-sufficient in food despite a doubling of its population. Finally, there is

China. For twenty years, from the late 1950s to the late 1970s, China stagnated economically and actually lost ground. Then, after the Cultural Revolution collapsed into chaos, the peasantry was given a little freedom to grow crops and to sell them on the market. Within five years farm production doubled.

This record of forty years of growth is unmatched in economic history. It even exceeds the records of the last fast-growth period, the forty years between 1875 and 1914. Then development moreover was confined to peoples of European stock. The United States and Germany became economic great powers. Austria-Hungary, northern Italy, and western Russia rapidly developed industrially; Argentina, Australia, New Zealand, Canada, and the Ukraine became major farm producers and exporters. The development of the last forty years from 1950 to the late 1980s has cut across any number of races and cultures. Quantitatively the development of these years certainly exceeds that of a hundred years ago. Then it embraced a fairly small segment of the human race—no more than one tenth. The development since World War II has embraced a fifth of the human race—even excluding the Chinese.

The Dismal Failures

Why then the widespread belief that development has been a dismal failure? The answer is that the successes were not at all what economists and politicians meant by "development" in the 1950s and 1960s. And what they expected and promised has indeed been a failure.

The "economic development" that was the great discovery of the fifties was to be universal and across the board. All countries, it was predicted, would develop and develop fast. In reality, development has been uneven and highly selective. The Communist world has, of course, not developed at all; on the contrary, it has "disdeveloped." But so have Argentina and Uruguay—both in 1950 far more developed than Brazil and far richer than Southern Europe. And a good deal of the Caribbean has equally "disdeveloped."

The development the economists and politicians promised was going to eliminate poverty. It was going to raise the incomes of the poor first and fastest. Instead, it everywhere first produced a new middle class. (Only in Japan is traditional poverty largely gone.) This is, of course, exactly what happened in every earlier period of economic development. This time, however—so we thought in the fifties and sixties—the poor would not have to wait. It was this promise, above all, that gave the development programs of those years—President Truman's Point Four in 1950 and President Kennedy's Alliance for Progress—their tremendous appeal. The development prophets of those years envisaged something like the America of 1950 or 1960 with its neat, single-family house for workers and a car in every garage. What they got—except in Japan—is very much like the America of 1920, when inequality seemed at its peak and poverty most shocking precisely because a large middle class had emerged. The defeat of poverty, we had to learn again, comes at the end and not at the beginning of economic development. In a modern society, poverty is far more a social than an economic condition, as witness the destitution in which one third of the blacks still live in the United States, the world's most highly developed country.

The fifties and sixties believed they had discovered economic development because they had new theories and new policies. These were widely acclaimed—though not all of them by the same people—as *guaranteeing* economic development. None has worked as advertised. There were four of these panaceas. The most widely touted has been the most abject failure: Soviet-style planning. By 1950 non-Communists already knew that it did not work in agriculture, but it was still widely believed that it was working in industry. Now we know that even in those years the Soviet figures for economic growth were largely figments of the bureaucratic imagination. Wherever tried, Soviet planning has produced only disdevelopment. If Russia had maintained growth at the pre-World War I rate, its industrial production would now equal or exceed that of the United States instead of being at most two fifths. The Russia of 1913, at least in its European areas, was on a par with the United States in health, infant mortality, and longevity. Seventy-five years later even European Russia is below most Third World countries in every single health category. Czechoslovakia, before it was made subject to Soviet planning (that is, before World War II), was the equal of West Germany in productivity and technology, and ahead of France. In World War II its industries were not damaged. Yet forty years after Soviet planning was imposed, Czech production per worker is less than half that of West Germany or of France. Cuba too produces a good deal less after thirty Communist years than it did before Castro. Then it was also way ahead of the rest of the Caribbean in health care and infant mortality. Now it is well behind everyone except Haiti.

One reason is the unbelievable waste and low productivity of capital investment under Soviet planning. Per dollar of investment the countries of the Communist bloc produce at best two fifths of what is produced in Western Europe, in the United States, or in Japan. But also the productivity of labor disappears under Soviet planning, if only because there is little point to working if there are no goods in the stores. And then—the fundamental flaw—"planning" inevitably misallocates resources and mismatches them.

Socialist non-Communist planning has done no better. Fashioned primarily in England during the thirties and forties at the London School of Economics, it has been the main cause of the catastrophic decline in production and productivity in the former British colonies in Africa. They were major food exporters before; all of them now have huge deficits in agricultural trade and would starve without food imports. India too only began to develop economically when the country's first prime minister, Jawaharlal Nehru, abandoned a few years before his death the Socialist planning he had brought back from his student days in England. And while Juan Perón may never have heard of the London School of Economics, the economic policies he imposed on Argentina in the 1950s were similar to those of the English theorists and had the same results: near-destruction of the country's flourishing agriculture; explosive growth of civilian and military bureaucracy; rampant corruption and raging inflation.

It was largely to counter the appeal of Soviet-style planning that President Truman proclaimed foreign aid as the American development policy. Unlike Soviet-style and Social Democratic planning, foreign aid has not led to wholesale disdevelopment. But it has not produced much development either. The analogy with the Marshall Plan on which it was based was simply not valid. Western Europe—and also Japan—had competence: educated and disciplined people, excellent schools, the infrastructure of transportation, of banking, of government, all of which are lacking in developing countries. Above all, the Marshall Plan worked with companies and industries. Foreign aid is aid to governments. As a result, a good deal of it became military aid, which, as we now know, hampers economic performance and development. Whatever aid went into economic investment went mainly into large prestige projects such as steel mills, which governments love. These are however more political showpieces than "multipliers" of human energies. They generate a lot of votes but little of the employment developing countries need the most: low-visibility and widely dispersed jobs for low-skilled people, in distribution and sales, in construction and road building, in automobile repair and gas stations, and in small local manufacturing. Such jobs are created in the main by small businesses satisfying local consumer wants rather than by heavy industry and the big projects that attract government aid.

Does Indicative Planning Work?

When it became apparent in the late sixties that neither Soviet-style planning nor Social Democratic planning nor foreign aid produced instant development, attention shifted to the one policy that did seem to work, the "indicative" planning of Charles de Gaulle's France and of "Japan Inc." In both countries government does not plan for business. It *indicates*—in close cooperation with business—where the economy should go. It then supports—primarily by directing investment to those industries and businesses that follow the "indicators." Despite all the publicity it enjoyed, indicative planning has failed in France. And it has had mixed results in Japan.

Indicative planning seemed to work in France for about ten years, until 1965 or so. Then it became apparent that all it actually did was to make France fall rapidly behind non-planning West Germany, France's rival for the leadership of Europe. Indicative planning stopped French industry from innovating, from exploiting opportunity and new technologies, and from exporting. Around 1970 it quietly died—and then France's economic growth began.

But "Japan Inc." is still held in awe. Actually what worked in Japan was not planning—that failed almost as badly as Soviet or Social Democratic planning did elsewhere. The Japanese government, with almost unfailing regularity, planned for the wrong targets. It did not plan the Japanese successes: the automobile industry, the consumer electronics industry, the photographic industry; in fact, it was opposed to the development of all three. Instead, the government pushed building up a huge steel industry—probably the most expensive mistake the Japanese have made. It has saddled their

147

country with about three times the steel capacity it can possibly sustain considering that Japan has neither iron ore, coal, natural gas, nor limestone. The industries that the Japanese government has been pushing since 1975 have also not been spectacularly successful. One prime target was large and larger supercomputers. But the market has shifted to the PC, the small, personal computer, which the Japanese government did not even have on its list. Japan has so far not developed a world-class pharmaceutical industry or, another prime government target, a world-class telecommunications industry. And it has only been moderately successful in office automation—the fourth of the government's targets. Only in microcircuits has the government plan attained its objectives.

The experience of Japan Inc. does teach one thing: the importance of close government-business relationships. These, however, work only if both government and business are already highly developed and competent. Otherwise—as the examples of India and Brazil show—the relationship will lead to cronyism and corruption rather than to policy and development. The Japanese lesson, in other words, is one for developed countries rather than for developing ones.

The Policies That Worked

The policies that did work in the last forty years were very different from those development economists and development politicians advocated. They were, however, equally different from those that had worked in the nineteenth century. Successful development in the nineteenth century was based on leadership in innovation and technology. Britain emerged as the first economic great power through leadership in steam engines, railroads, and steamships; textile machines and machine tools; international banking and insurance; and communications (e.g., the Post Office). The United States then became the next economic great power through leadership in steel, electricity, telegraphy and telephony; farm equipment and agronomy; office equipment such as the typewriter; and the first household appliance, the sewing machine. And the United States soon added leadership in automobiles and aviation. Germany at the same time emerged—in competition with the United States—as a leader in steel, electricity, electronics, and telegraphy. It became the innovator in chemicals and pharmaceuticals, in automobiles, and in banking with the invention of the "universal bank." The Japanese did not even try to attain technological or scientific leadership in any one area. So far, the Japanese development has primarily been based on imported science and on improving other people's technology.

The two policies that did work in the forty years after World War II were exporting the products of low-wage industrial labor and "infant-industry protection." Both had indeed been tried in the nineteenth century; in fact, they may be considered the first systematic and purposeful development policies. But both failed totally and had to be abandoned. Economists and industrialists soon learned in the nineteenth century that low-wage labor is unproductive and low-quality labor, and cannot compete on the world markets. This was still true in the twenties and thirties when the Japanese desperately tried to penetrate the world markets with products made by low-cost labor. The failure of their export drive helped persuade Japanese policy makers to try military conquest to obtain the markets they could not penetrate by using low-wage labor.

Then, after World War II, the Japanese realized that *training,* an American invention, makes workers highly productive while still remaining low-wage. Export-led development, based on low-wage but highly trained labor that produced quality goods, became the means by which Japan pulled itself out of underdevelopment and defeat. The strategy was copied by the other Far Eastern developing countries, South Korea, Hong Kong, Taiwan, Singapore, and, to some extent, by Brazil.

The Japanese, having become high-wage producers themselves, are now moving labor-intensive work into Thailand, Malaya, and to plants (the so-called *maquiladoras*) on the Mexican side of the U.S. border. But this is probably the last gasp of the low labor-cost policy. It works only as long as industrial manufacturing is labor-intensive. When direct labor costs fall below 15 percent of total cost, the expenses of distance such as freight charges begin to outweigh the advantages of low wages. Nowadays, it is a backward industry in which direct labor costs are that high. At General Motors direct labor costs still account for around 25 percent of the total costs of a car; but at Toyota and Ford they are down to 18 percent and are expected to be no more than 10 or 12 percent before the end of this century. Even in operations that have always been highly labor-intensive, such as the assembly of radios or computers, direct labor costs are already well below 20 percent by now and still falling. There will always be manufacturing operations with higher labor costs—e.g., sewing men's suits or assembling wooden furniture. But they are far too few in number and employ too few people to be the launching pad for economic development as they were for the Far East in the decades after 1950.

Indeed, the Japanese realized early on that low-labor-cost exports would not carry them very long. By 1960 they had combined the low-wage strategy with a new version of the nineteenth century's other unsuccessful development strategy, infant-industry protection. The invention of America's perennial presidential candidate, Henry Clay (he called it "the American System"), it was taken to Europe by a German, Georg Friedrich List, who as a political exile in the United States had been Clay's secretary. Infant-industry protection at first was all the rage. It soon became a disappointment. To protect its infant industries, a country closes its borders to manufacturing imports; in theory it then opens its borders again when the infants are strong enough to withstand competition. But that never happens. On the contrary, the longer the infants are protected, the more dependent they become on even more protection. But also the more domestic industry grows under "infant-industry protection," the more dependent it becomes on imports of machinery, tools, industrial materials, and components from the more highly developed countries. In the end the infant industries can neither grow further without constantly increased imports of machinery and components, nor export competitively to earn the foreign exchange needed to pay for these machines and components. In the end the very growth of the infant industries defeats them.

This is what has happened to Mexico—this century's most assiduous practitioner of infant-industry protection. The policy shielded Mexican manufacturers so that they grew fast. But the more they grew, the less competitive they became, while at the same time requiring ever-increasing supplies from abroad, especially industrial materials and spare parts. For a few years when OPEC drove petroleum prices sky-high, petroleum exports provided the foreign exchange Mexican industry needed to buy spare parts and technology from abroad. Then, for a few short years, Mexico borrowed heavily abroad. When that came to an end, the Mexican economy came crashing down.

India, the other major practitioner of infant-industry protection, has been a great deal more prudent than Mexico. As a result it has grown much less fast. But in the end it faces the same dilemma. Indian factories have steadily become less rather than more competitive. At the same time they have become increasingly dependent on imports of machinery, spare parts, and components—without the export capacity to pay for them. India too is in danger of succumbing to the "infant-industry crisis" that made nineteenth-century countries such as Germany abandon the policy as suicidal in the not-so-long run.

The Japanese, who found a way around the limitations of low-wage competition, also found—or thought they did—a way around the limitations of infant-industry protection. They combined the nineteenth century's two failed policies: low-wage labor exports and infant-industry protection. This gave Japan's industries both the high prices and high profits of a protected home market and the competitive challenge and foreign-exchange earnings of the world market. For thirty years this combination of infant-industry protection at home and competitive exporting on the world market worked for Japan. It has worked for South Korea. It also became the policy on which Brazil based its development. All three have grown spectacularly. In the end, however, the strategy fails. As has already been explained, it leads to adversarial trade sooner or later—and from now on it will always be sooner. The developed countries then soon refuse to accept imports from a country to which they cannot export, whatever the reasons or excuses. Perhaps more important, the infant industries still do not grow up—or rather, only those that are major exporters do. The others—they are always the majority—become just as dependent on further protection and just as deformed and stunted as if the country did not export at all. And thus the country becomes increasingly unwilling, even unable, to do without protection. To do so would threaten massive bankruptcies, heavy unemployment, and economic crisis.

Indeed, fear is the main reason why Japan so tenaciously resists the pressures to open up its economy. Too many businesses and industries would be endangered. Only the active exporters are competitive; and they constitute less than an eighth of the total of Japanese manufacturing industry. The rest, in manufacturing as well as in services, cannot compete and are dependent on protection. Even most of the exporters need the high prices they charge the domestic customer to support the lower prices they get overseas. The same situation—in more extreme form—prevails in Brazil and South Korea.

There has never been a more successful economic policy than the one Japan has followed since 1960. But it is nearing a dead end. The developed countries have caught on. The European Economic Community is mobilizing itself against Japanese (and Korean) imports. The United States, while still trying to persuade Japan to open its markets to goods and services from America, is also threatening to close American markets to the Japanese, to Brazil, to Korea. From now on the developed countries will increasingly practice reciprocity, which stalemates export-led, infant-industry protection.

The End of the Development Promise

We may be at the end of the development era that began almost forty years ago with President Truman's Point Four. Indeed, it is being argued that all that matters is the "Triad,"* the developed countries of North America, Western Europe, and the Far East, and that we can disregard both the Communist world and the "Third World" of developing non-Communist countries. The Triad countries do indeed produce more food than they themselves consume and practically all the industrial raw materials they need. They also produce and consume two thirds of the world's manufactured goods.

But a tremendous development potential exists—and we know how to convert it into reality. Communist China demonstrated this when it ever so slightly relaxed control of farmers and farm prices in the seventies—and farm production doubled within a few years. The greatest opportunities for development now lie in undoing the policies that have not worked,

*A term coined by the Japanese management consultant Kenichi Ohmae.

and especially Communist-style planning and Social Democrat planning. The potential, as Chinese farming has shown,
is very large. But it will be excruciatingly difficult politically,
socially, and economically to take the necessary actions. The
Chinese Communists learned that development requires a
market economy. Yet no Chinese leader can have forgotten
that it was not Mao who defeated Chiang Kai-shek; it was
inflation, which lost Chiang the support of both the urban
workers and his armies. And thus the Chinese did not dare lift
price controls on staples such as rice, wheat, and pork. The
predictable outcome of maintaining these controls was that
five years later peasants no longer grew enough wheat, rice,
and pork to feed the urban masses, so rationing had to be
reintroduced. Otherwise the regime might not have lasted—
dictatorships do not long survive urban food riots. Can the
Chinese Communists free manufacturing industry, no matter
how great the gains in production, efficiency, and quality, if
it means large-scale unemployment in the big cities on
China's sea coast? Reversing the self-defeating policies of
Communist China, however, may still be easier than to free
African peasants from the Social Democratic planning that
has destroyed their incentives to grow anything at all. This
would require letting food prices rise sharply in the big cities
with their huge, and politically volatile, slums. And can Chairman Gorbachev do much more than *talk* economic reform?

To restore the growth capacity of the newly industrializing
countries of the non-Communist world—Brazil, Mexico,
India—should be easier and fully as rewarding. They now
have the foundation for productive and competitive industry.
Whatever need there might have been for infant-industry protection is gone. But the change requires great political cour-
age. The transition might be so painful as to endanger social
and political cohesion. This predictably is going to be a central problem of the Third World for years, if not decades, to

come. Recovery rather than development is thus likely to be the priority for the coming years. It is a problem of the political will rather than one of economics.

Still there are those pictures of President Kennedy hanging in the peasant huts from Mexico to Patagonia. "Development" will not be forgotten. We now know that it is not easy. We know that it is not fast. We know that it first makes poverty more visible and harder to accept—precisely because it first develops a middle class. We know that it means hard work rather than foreign aid. We know that there is no formula and no one policy that can be guaranteed to work. We know that its foundations are education and competence rather than capital investment. It is not a "sure thing" but risky. It cannot be provided; it must be achieved. But the successes of the last forty years show that it can be achieved.

11

ECONOMICS AT THE CROSSROADS

No existing economic theory explains the main economic events of the fifteen years between 1975 and 1989. Nor could it have predicted them. Reality has outgrown existing theories. This has happened twice before. First, in the years of the "divide" of the 1870s. Then the "neoclassicists," Karl Menger in Austria, William Stanley Jevons in England, and Léon Walras in France, created modern economics with their "marginal-utility" theory. Sixty years later, when the Great Depression confounded neoclassical theory, John Maynard Keynes created a new synthesis, the economic theory of the nation-state, in which the neoclassicists' marginal-utility theory is a subset, a "building block" rechristened "microeconomics." Since then, there have been only minor adjustments. Milton Friedman and the supply siders must be seen as "post-Keynesian rather than "anti-Keynesian."

Keynes, the post-Keynesians, and the neoclassicists alike cast the economy in a model in which a few constants drive the entire machinery. The model we now need would have to see the economy as "ecology," "environment," "configuration," and as composed of several interacting spheres: a "microeconomy" of individuals and firms, especially transnational ones; a "macroeconomy" of national governments; and a world economy. Every earlier economic theory postulated that one such economy totally controls; all others are dependent and "functions." In the marginal-utility world of the neoclassicists, the microeconomy of individuals and firms controls the macroeconomy of government. In the Keynesian and post-Keynesian worlds, the macroeconomy of national money and credit controls the microeconomy of individuals and firms. But economic reality now is one of three such economies. And soon the economic region (as in the European Economic Community), may become a fourth semi-dependent economy. Each, to use a mathematician's term, is a partially dependent variable. None totally controls the other three; none is totally controlled by the others. Yet none is fully independent from the others, either. Such complexity can barely be described. It cannot be analyzed since it allows of no prediction.

To give us a functioning economic theory, we thus need a new synthesis that simplifies—but so far there is no sign of it. And if no such synthesis emerges, we may be at the end of economic theory. There may then be only economic *theorems,* that is, formulae and formulations that describe or explain this or that phenomenon and solve this or that problem rather than presenting economics as a coherent system. But there also then would be no "economic policy" as the term is now understood, that is, no foundation for governmental action to manage the business cycle and economic conditions altogether.

Economic policy requires that lay people such as politicians understand the key concepts of economic theory. But economic reality is much too complex for that. It is already difficult, if not impossible, to give answers understandable to a lay person to the simplest economic question. If there is not

157

again a simple economic theory—or at least one capable of simplification—then there can be only "economic policies" aimed at a specific problem, such as an inadequate savings rate. There can be only what might be called "economic hygiene" or "preventive economics." These would aim at strengthening the basic health of an economy so that it could resist even severe bouts of economic crisis rather than at curing a crisis or managing it.

Economic Realities

Here are some of the realities of the last fifteen years, the years since the mid-seventies, which no economic theory could have predicted or can explain.

At the beginning of the period, President Jimmy Carter pushed down the foreign-exchange value of the American dollar from 250 to 180 yen to the dollar. He did this to promote American exports and thereby create jobs—America's unemployment rate was high and climbing. President Carter succeeded in triggering a record rise in exports, but it did not reduce unemployment. On the contrary, unemployment rose steadily despite an export boom. This is something no economist would have predicted or can explain. Even less explainable: during this period of fast-rising unemployment, when logically there should have been deflation and falling prices, dangerous inflation set in, with the fever reaching highs of 12 and 14 percent a year.

When Ronald Reagan succeeded President Carter, he raised interest rates sharply to stop inflation. He did indeed get rid of inflation fast. But the high interest rates also pushed the dollar back up to a 250 rate against the yen. This severely damaged American exports, especially of farm products, while at the same time creating an unprecedented market in the United States for industrial imports, especially from Japan. According to all economic theory, there should have been substantial unemployment. Instead, the unemployment rate during the Reagan administration went down to the lowest level in fourteen years, that is, since before President Carter. When President Reagan left office in January 1989, the United States had over-full employment in most areas and acute labor shortages.

In the fall of 1985, President Reagan abruptly reversed course. He began to talk down the dollar just as President Carter had done eight years earlier. President Reagan's economists aimed at a "slight correction" of an "overvalued currency," maybe from 250 to 220 yen per dollar. Instead, the dollar went into "free fall" and was down to 125 yen sixteen months later. According to all economic theory—but also according to all earlier precedents—there should have been a massive "flight from the dollar." Foreigners holding dollars—and by that time Japan, West Germany, Taiwan, and Canada, the main exporters to the United States, had all accumulated huge holdings of U.S. government obligations denominated in dollars—should have scrambled to limit their foreign-exchange losses by reducing their dollar holdings. Instead, all of them—especially the Japanese—increased their lending to the United States and in U.S. dollars.

To confound economic theory even further, the U.S. dollar prices of raw materials—from wheat to cotton and from petroleum to copper—did not go up at all in dollars. Their *dollar prices* actually went further down, which meant in effect that for all but the Americans raw material prices in their currencies were cut by more than half—for Arab petroleum producers, for Rhodesian copper mine owners, for Danish butter exporters, for the Japanese. At that, food and raw material prices were already at depression lows in 1985, even in overvalued dollars. The devaluation of the dollar should immediately have raised the dollar prices of goods imported by America. But the Japanese did something totally unprecedented. To maintain sales in the American market, they maintained their prices in the United States which, of course, meant that they took a 50 percent cut in their own currency in what they received for their exports.

What happened in Japan was equally unprecedented and can also not be explained by any known economic theory. The large Japanese companies sharply raised the prices for their products on the home market so as to compensate for the drop in income from America. This, all economic theory would say, must create recession. Instead, it triggered the wildest consumer boom in Japan's history. The only explanation offered is that there has been a generation change in Japan. The baby-boomers are now reaching middle age and are emulating the West in their desire for immediate material gratification. But economically speaking this explanation is nonsense. The generation change should have had exactly the opposite effect according to the one theory regarding savings and spending that economists of all persuasions have come to accept, the "life cycle" savings theory (for which Franco Modigliani, its discoverer, had received the Nobel Prize in Economics just a year earlier, in 1985). The theory would have predicted a rise in the savings rate rather than in consumption.

Actually all along since the early seventies, reality and the available economic theories had been moving further and further apart. *And we know why.*

The Economic Model and Its Assumptions

The economic theory model assumes first that the controlling economy is that of the sovereign state. Individuals and firms had been the masters in the economic model of the neoclassicists. In prevailing economics—Keynesian and post-Keynesian—the microeconomy is, so to speak, the "servant quarter"; and the servants do as they are told by their new master, the macroeconomy.

Secondly, before Keynes, economists asserted that the "real" economy of goods and services was the controlling factor. Marx called money the "veil of reality." For the Keynesians and post-Keynesians, money *is* reality. Control of the quantity of money in the economy totally controls the behavior of goods and services. It totally controls the "servants," the individuals and the firms in the microeconomy.

Finally, contemporary economic theories assume that the only economy that matters—indeed, the only one that exists—is the national economy. To be sure, they recognize economic transactions across boundaries. But these are controlled by managing the internal economy of the national state.

Every one of these axiomatic assumptions flies in the face of reality. Individuals and firms never submitted to their supposed master, the macroeconomy; from the beginning, they successfully sabotaged. And there are events in the microeconomy which profoundly affect the macroeconomy but which money, credit, interest rates, taxes do not control and do not even greatly influence. But also there now is a world economy.

The Economy as a "Perfect Gas"

Keynes himself likened the economy of the sovereign national state to the perfect gas of physics. Molecules in the gas can be seen to move, often quite violently—the so-called Brownian motion. But the motion is random and accidental; it is without impact on the gas itself. The only thing that matters in a perfect gas are temperature and pressure, neither of which is affected by the particles' Brownian motion. Similarly, individuals and firms may look as though they are making decisions and acting, but this is pure delusion. All that individuals and firms can do is to *re-*act. Any attempt to act contrary to the realities of money, interest rates, and credit is futile and self-defeating. Money, credit, interest rates are to the national economy what temperature and pressure are to the perfect gas.

Keynes assumed that the velocity of the turnover of money—the technical term for how fast individuals spend their money—was a "social habit" that remains unchanged over long periods, barring catastrophic events. But as Joseph Schumpeter pointed out in the mid-thirties, the evidence shows clearly that individuals are capable of changing the velocity of the turnover of their money—fast, unexpectedly, and quite independent of economic policy. In fact, the ability of individuals and firms to change the velocity of money turnover has defeated every single attempt at economic control through government policy these last sixty years. By 1936, the New Deal had pumped enormous amounts of purchasing power into the pockets of American consumers. This should have revived the economy. But consumers chose not to spend their additional purchasing power; they hoarded the money instead. This caused the economy to collapse in 1936–37, with unemployment again as high as it had been four years earlier when Roosevelt was inaugurated. The individual's ability to control the velocity of the turnover of money also explains why President Carter's policy was a disaster. Consumers did not spend and create jobs; they hoarded. In a rapid reversal, American consumers then spent, and indeed increased their spending during the Reagan presidency, which explains in large measure why President Reagan's policy worked despite the large trade deficit. Economists confronted with these facts blame "confidence." But if any government ever had the public's confidence it was Franklin D. Roosevelt's first administration. Furthermore, it is precisely confidence that the contemporary economic theories, whether Keynesian or post-Keynesian, promise to deliver.

The way the Japanese manufacturers reacted to the drop in the exchange value of the American dollar and to the resulting drop in their export earnings spotlights a second area where the microeconomic servants, the individuals and firms, are in control and the masters. They, rather than the macroeconomy, decide what is economically "rational." The economist defines economic "rationality" as "profit maximization." But over what time period? For the individual transaction, that is, for every single automobile shipped from Toyota's Nagoya plant to the United States? For the current quarter of the accounting year, or for any other accounting period? Or for the lifetime of the investment—eight or ten years in the case of an automobile plant? All of these are equally "rational." And as the example of the Japanese exporters shows, the answer to the question of what time period is appropriate is a "decision" rather than a "reaction" on the part of individual and firm. In fact, as every businessman could have told the economists, the decision between short-term and long-term results is the single most important decision top management in a business is being paid for, the most difficult one, the most controversial one—and anything but a foregone conclusion. The Japanese story shows that the decision profoundly affects—indeed, it largely molds—the national macroeconomy. The economist, however, has nothing to say on how to make this decision, nor does he have any way to allow for it in his model.

Finally, there is no room in contemporary economic theory for technology, for innovation, for change altogether. Like their predecessors, the neoclassicists, economists postulate an unchanging economy, an economy in equilibrium. Technology, innovation, and change are external. Economists know, of course, that technology, innovation, and change matter. They have even made several attempts to bring technology and change into their model. These have all failed, and for the same reason: there is very little, if any, correlation between monetary policy, credit, and interest rates on the one hand and entrepreneurship, invention, and innovation on the other. Whatever controls the latter, it is independent of the macroeconomy. And yet entrepreneurships, invention, and innovation can change the economy in a remarkably short time. They, rather than the macro-economy, are the master.

World Economy and Economic Theory

A functioning economic theory thus needs to integrate three spheres: the macroeconomy of money, credit, and interest rates; the microeconomic decisions on the velocity of the turnover of money and on the time period that is the "now" of economic decisions; and entrepreneurship and innovation.

If this were not enough, there is a new and even more daunting challenge: the transnational world economy. The world economy has become a reality, and one largely separate from national economies. The world economy strongly affects national economies; in extreme circumstances it controls them. The world economy controlled President Mitterand's France in 1981 and forced it to reverse course after only one hundred eighty days of Socialist policies. The world economy at all times sets stringent limits to the macroeconomy, especially in respect to money, credit, and interest rates.

Economic "rationality" differs in the world economy, and with it the time periods for economic decisions. For some decisions, time spans in the world economy are very short—for example, in trading currencies or commodities. But for business decisions—as against trading decisions—the time periods of the world economy are long. When President Reagan raised the value of the American dollar in the early 1980s, American exporters decided to maintain their profit margins in dollars by raising prices for foreigners buying American goods. They defined "profit maximization" in terms of months. It was the wrong decision. Very soon the Americans began to lose overseas sales; within two years they had lost profitability altogether. The Japanese, four years later, learning from the mistake of the Americans, decided to maintain their markets in America at the expense of their profit margins. This actually maximized their profits. They were again making money by the end of two years. "Sales" in the world market are not sales; they are returns on long-term investment. What matters is the total return over the lifetime of the investment. This is, of course, also "profit maximization." But it is not what microeconomic theory means by the term.

Economics and the Mathematics of Complexity

It is not only reality that challenges the economic model we currently have to work with. A subtle but potentially equally serious challenge to the theoretical foundations and the methodology of economics is on the horizon.

In the 1870s Léon Walras in France made economics into a "hard" science by casting it into a mathematical mold. There have been countless changes and additions since. But Walras's mathematics still provides the logic of economics, the methodology of economics, and the assumptions regarding the character of economics. It is a mechanical model that uses the mathematics of nineteenth-century physics (which, of course, was all that was available in Walras's time). In a mechanical model it is assumed that the *statistically significant* matters and determines. This, however, has now been shown to be a dubious assumption for the kind of world with which economics deals.

The fastest-growing field of modern mathematics is the theory of complexity. It shows, with rigorous, mathematical proof, that complex systems do not allow prediction; they are controlled by factors that are not statistically significant. This has become known as the "butterfly effect": a whimsical but mathematically rigorous (and experimentally proven) theorem shows that a butterfly flapping its wings in the Amazon rain forest can and does control the weather in Chicago a few weeks or months later. In complex systems, the "climate" is predictable and has high stability; the "weather" is not predictable and is totally unstable. And no complex system can

165

exclude anything as "external." In respect to the weather, that is, in respect to short-term phenomena, there is no system. There is only chaos.

Economics and economic policy deal with short-term phenomena. They deal with recessions and with change in prices. Contemporary economics and economic policy assume that the system, the long term, is made by short-term policies, for example, changes in interest rates, government spending, tax rates, and so on. For a complex system this is simply not true, as modern mathematics has now proven. And this explains also why so many of the government policies of the post–World War II period have not worked. The Chicago economist George J. Stigler (winner of the 1982 Nobel Prize in Economics) has shown in years of painstaking research that not one of the regulations through which the U.S. government has tried over the years to control, direct, or regulate the economy has worked. They either were ineffectual or they produced the opposite of the intended results. Stigler had no explanation; we now know that this is precisely how the "butterfly effect" works—and will work again. The "butterfly effect" is also the only explanation for the Japanese consumer boom of 1986 and 1987.

In any system as complex as the economy of a developed country, the statistically insignificant events, the events at the margin, are likely to be the decisive events, short range at least. By definition they can neither be anticipated nor prevented. Indeed, they cannot always be identified even after they have had their impact.

From Economic Theory to Economic Theorems

The last fifty years, and especially those since World War II, have been years of great progress and productivity in economics. We have a good deal of solid knowledge now about specifics. We know, for instance, quite a bit about productivity—the very term was virtually unknown sixty years ago. We know a good deal about the cost of union work rules and union restrictions, and about their impact on quality. We know far more than we did thirty years ago about corporation finance and about pricing. But we have no new synthesis, nothing that could remotely compare to the work done by Jevons, Menger, and Walras more than a hundred years ago, or by Keynes sixty years ago.

Such a synthesis may not be possible, however badly it is needed—at least not in the form of a scientific theory. An equation with many partially dependent variables cannot be solved, as any mathematics beginner is taught. To have a genuine economic theory would therefore require *one* new unifying principle that predicts and controls economic behavior in all four economies: the microeconomy of individuals and firms; the macroeconomy of the national state; the economy of transnational businesses; and the world economy. Without such a unifying principle, economics could give us only theoretical explanations of specific events and answers to specific problems. It could not give us a theory of the economy. This is perfectly respectable. It is, after all, what medicine became when, around the year 1700, it abandoned the search for both an all-embracing theory of vital processes and a universal cureall. It is what engineering has been all along. But it is something very different from what economists have been trying for in their attempts for more than a century to fashion their discipline in the image of a true natural science such as physics.

From "Weather" to "Climate"

The new mathematics of complexity raises an even more disturbing question: Can there be an economic policy at all? Or is the attempt to control the "weather" of the economy, such as recessions and other cyclical fluctuations, foredoomed to failure?

Economics rose to its eminence in this century precisely

because it promised to be able to control the "weather." Prior to 1929, no government had ever attempted to do this, nor did popular opinion expect it to do so. But when the Great Depression swept the world in the early thirties, the demand for an activist government arose. Keynes was ready with a theory which asserted for the first time that government could indeed manage and control the economy. The results have hardly met the tests of efficacy and safety we apply to a new drug before it is approved for medical practice.

We are unlikely to absolve government from responsibility for the economic weather. Elections will be won and lost by the voters' appraisal of a government's economic performance. But are we going to shift from government as the economic activist of the last sixty years to emphasis on government responsibility to maintain the right "climate"?

An analogy would be the manner in which the physician dealt with bacterial pneumonia before the coming of antibiotics: keep the patient warm, give him plenty of bed rest and fluids, and make him as comfortable as possible, thus allowing a reasonably healthy body a chance to fight the infection. Another analogy would be the manner in which today's physician preaches "prevention": "keep fit, keep your weight down, don't smoke, don't drink."

Indeed, the politicians whom today's voters support most strongly are moving toward policies that create the climate, and away from trying to control the weather. Margaret Thatcher, as prime minister of Great Britain since 1979, has been treating her country's severe economic ills very much the way yesterday's physician treated pneumonia. West Germany has followed even longer a policy of conservation rather than of intervention. "If in doubt, do nothing" has been the German maxim. The Japanese economic policy since the late fifties has also focused on the climate, on creating and maintaining the right conditions for a strong and healthy economy.

There are signs of such a shift toward climate in the concerns of economic policy. We talk increasingly about economic structure: productivity, competitiveness, long-term versus short-term management perspectives, industry mix, the role and organization of research, government-business relations, the right industrial relations, and so on. None of these concerns has a place in our economic theories or in the economists' models of the economy. Nor can the mathematics of economic theory handle any of these factors. Even productivity is so heavily qualitative as not to be quantifiable with any precision. Yet these are the determinants of economic reality. They, rather than short-term cyclical fluctuations, are what decides "the wealth of nations."

What economists consider to be "economics" is bound to change. "Whoever argues impact on jobs," goes an old economists' saying, "rather than impact on the consumer, is not an economist but a politician." Since modern economics emerged, in the 1870s, benefit to the consumer—especially in the form of lower prices and with them greater purchasing power and increasing consumer choice—has been the touchstone of economic policy for economists. The argument for excluding or at least subordinating everything else is indeed a strong one. Any blurring in the name of jobs or production of the focus on the consumer as the sole object of economics abets price fixing, monopoly, and inefficiency. It soon endangers jobs rather than protecting them. This identification of economic rationality with the consumer interest was powerfully reinforced by Keynesian and post-Keynesian theory, which asserts that it is primarily consumer buying that creates investment, productive capacity, and wealth.

Economic policy in every country has, of course, never eliminated concern for jobs, let along protection of producer interests. But increasingly the impacts of economic policy on a country's or an industry's productivity and competitiveness will also have to be taken seriously by economic theory. The success in Japan, in South Korea, but also in West Germany, of policies to bolster a country's competitive position that deliberately subordinate the consumer to the producer has been far too great to be brushed aside as something that should not have happened. And the economists' assumption that long-range, wealth-producing capacity automatically results from maximizing a large number of short-range consumer benefits carries little intellectual conviction in an era of rapid change and innovation. From now on, increasingly, the short-term focus on the consumer will have to be balanced by a long-term concern with productivity and competitiveness.

The ideal policy would optimize both. The best we can hope for is probably policies that balance the two, with each limiting the other. Consumer benefit is the goal as long as its pursuit does not significantly impair productivity and competitiveness. Productivity and competitiveness are the goals as long as their pursuit demands only minor consumer sacrifices. Such a policy—difficult enough under the best of circumstances—would be politically almost impossible unless buttressed by a clear theory that shows how to calculate the tradeoffs. Such a theory, as already said, would have to be able to integrate the technical complexities this chapter has tried to describe into a simple unifying model capable of analysis.

So far we do not have even the beginnings of such a theory.

PART IV

THE NEW KNOWLEDGE
SOCIETY

12

THE POST-BUSINESS SOCIETY

The biggest shift—bigger by far than the changes in politics, government, or economics—is the shift to the knowledge society in all developed non-Communist countries. Here are some of its important features.

The social center of gravity has shifted to the knowledge worker. All developed countries are becoming post-business, knowledge societies. Access to good jobs and career opportunities in developed countries increasingly requires a university diploma.

Looked at one way, this is the logical result of a long evolution in which we moved from working by the sweat of our brow and by muscle to industrial work and finally to knowledge work. But the development also represents a sharp break with the past. Until quite recently there were few jobs requiring knowledge. Knowledge was ornament rather than necessity. Only one of America's business builders in the nineteenth century had any advanced schooling: J. P. Morgan, the great financier. And he was a college dropout, leaving Göttingen University, where he had gone to study mathemat-

173

ics, to become a trainee in a small bank. Very few of the other prominent business figures of the nineteenth century even entered high school, let alone graduated from it. Knowledge work began to expand—and fast—in the twentieth century. The American population has tripled in this century, from 75 million in 1900 to 250 million now. But college teachers grew from fewer than 10,000 at the beginning of the century—most of them teaching in small church schools—to more than 500,-000 eighty years later. All other categories of knowledge workers grew at similar rates—accountants, physicians, medical technologists, analysts of all kinds, managers, and so on. And the trend in other developed countries closely parallels the United States.

• The shift to knowledge and education as the passport to good jobs and career opportunities means, above all, a shift from a society in which business was the main avenue of advancement to a society in which business is only one of the available opportunities and no longer a distinct one. *It represents a shift to the post-business society.* The shift has gone furthest in the United States and in Japan, but it is also in train in most of Western Europe.

• Even in the decades following World War II when college enrollments exploded and knowledge rapidly became the economy's foundation and its true "capital," the quickest and easiest road to a good job and to job security in developed countries was not through education. It was going at age seventeen into the unionized mass-production factory as a semi-skilled worker. A year later—often sooner—that worker earned more in all developed countries (excepting only Japan) than the holder of a university degree could expect to earn for fifteen or twenty years. Even then the semi-skilled mass-production worker had higher job security after fifteen or twenty years of service than the college graduate, except for government servants and tenured teaching faculty. But now the center of gravity in society is shifting to a new group—the knowledge worker—who has new values and expectations. The blue-collar workers in manufacturing industry, who registered the most spectacular advances in income and social status during the first three quarters of this century, are becoming the "other half" and a "social problem." They are becoming a "counterculture" rather than "mainstream." Whether the industrial workers' own institution, the labor union, can survive, and in what capacity, also is becoming problematical.

• Another "counterculture" is emerging in the United States: the third sector of non-profit, non-governmental institutions with their "unpaid staff" of volunteers.

• Management has emerged as both central social function and a new and distinctive liberal art. But this raises the question of management's legitimacy. And organizations are evolving into new forms; they are becoming information-based.

• That knowledge has become the capital of a developed economy, and knowledge workers the group that sets society's values and norms, finally affects what we mean by knowledge and how it is learned and taught.

Business Has Succeeded Too Well

Forty years ago, after World War II, business was still a dirty word for "intellectuals" everywhere. Even in the United States top-flight university graduates turned up their noses at business jobs and tried instead to get into government service or university teaching. Now grandmothers give the latest business best seller instead of a Bible to their grandsons as a high-school graduation present. The pastor of an evangelical church—though he considers himself "anti-business"—is as conversant with cash-flow analysis as any accountant and runs it off routinely on his personal computer. He attends management seminars to learn how to maintain "spiritual entre-

175

preneurship" as the chief executive officer of his fast-growing congregation. Communist Party leaders sing the praises of the profit motive and of market competition. And photographs of "raiders" juggling billions in successful hostile takeovers, instead of those of scantily clad models, adorn the covers of popular magazines.

Business has been the success story of the post-World War II period—something very few people would have dreamed of in the thirties or during World War II. Thirty-five years ago "business" was still widely viewed as an anachronism to be engulfed everywhere in a rising socialist tide. But socialism has become the anachronism. Instead of capitalism being a transition stage on the socialist road, it now increasingly appears that socialism is a detour on the capitalist road.

The forty years since World War II saw an unprecedented expansion of production and productivity, world trade, and world investment. During these forty years, the business school—once the poor relation of higher education and openly sneered at in most respectable institutions—has grown everywhere and has become the biggest single faculty in large universities worldwide. Even Oxford now has a management college and features management studies.

This success is precisely what is weakening—"sapping" may not be too strong a word—business as a distinct culture. All institutions —government agencies, the military, churches (at least in the U.S.), hospitals, museums, the Boy Scouts— have become "management-conscious." Indeed, they owe their growth and impact in the United States very largely to their adoption of, and leadership in, management. But these institutions see in management a tool to carry out their own mission and to be as different as possible from a business. In some cases such institutions even adopt the legal guise of a profit-making entity so as to better function as a "non-business." And schools of business are rapidly changing their name to schools of management to emphasize that the business concepts and business skills they teach are applicable, are indeed needed, for any organized purposeful activity in society. Meanwhile in business proper, the values of business are no longer held with conviction and commitment.

The business society is still in full bloom in the rapidly industrializing countries, the countries that are moving from "developing" to being "developed." This can be seen in São Paulo, in Singapore, in Hong Kong, and can be discerned, just beneath the surface, in post-Mao China. Mr. Deng's remark about China in 1985, "Getting rich is beautiful," was made in a developed country a hundred and fifty years earlier, by Louis-Philippe, the last Bourbon king of France. The business society flourishes among the Asian immigrants, the Koreans, Thai, and Vietnamese, who are streaming into southern California and starting family-owned grocery stores, ethnic restaurants, and laundromats so that their children can go to college and become doctors and lawyers. If Mikhail Gorbachev succeeds in his attempt to restore economic momentum to that singularly "underdeveloped" country, the Soviet Union, a genuine business society will surely arise there too.

Where business has succeeded, in the developed non-Communist world, it has succeeded so well that we can increasingly afford to satisfy what have always been considered "non-business," indeed, "non-economic" wants. In this century, business has increased the capacity to produce wealth explosively—at least twenty times in the major non-Communist developed countries and perhaps even faster in some of the developing ones such as South Korea, Brazil, or Spain. No more than one third of this has gone into the production of material goods. Half of the expansion in wealth-producing capacity was used to create leisure time by cutting the hours worked while steadily increasing pay. An American worker now puts in 1,800 hours a year as compared to 3,300 hours in the early years of the century. The cut has been as large in

Japan, where the hours worked have gone down from 3,500 in the early years of the century to around 2,000 a year now. In Europe the cut has been even greater, especially in West Germany, where working hours a year are down to not much more than 1,500.

An additional third of the increased wealth-producing capacity has gone into health care, where expenditures have gone from less than 1 percent of gross national product to 8–11 percent (depending on the country) in fifty years. There has been almost equal growth—from 2 percent of GNP to 10–11 percent—in the expenditures on formal schooling; and with more and more schooling taking place outside the formal school system, especially in and by employing institutions, the proportion of GNP that now goes to education is much higher than the 10 percent officially reported. Leisure, health care, and schooling require goods; they are not spiritual. Very little of the new leisure is used for intellectual pursuits. The free hours are more likely to be spent in front of the television set watching "Dallas" or sports. Still, neither leisure nor health care nor education were ever considered economic satisfactions. They represent values quite different from those of the "business society." They bespeak a society in which economic satisfactions are a means rather than a good in themselves, and in which business therefore is a tool rather than a way of life.

The Decline of the Capitalist

As a result of the success of business, the capitalist has become economically almost irrelevant in developed countries. He has both far less economic power and far less political power than he had before World War I. Then, great businessmen—a John D. Rockefeller, a J. P. Morgan, an Andrew Carnegie, an Alfred Krupp—could finance entire industries out of their own pockets. They were indeed Marx's capitalists, who own and control the means of production. The total wealth of America's one thousand richest people today (according to figures in the September 9, 1988, *Fortune* Magazine) would barely cover the capital needs of one major American industry for a few months. The employees through their pension funds are now the capitalists. Indeed, no one today, not even the fattest oil sheik or the richest Japanese real-estate billionaire, has as large a fortune (adjusted for inflation and taxes) as had each of the "tycoons" of 1900. If all the "super-rich" of the developed countries suddenly disappeared, the world economy would not even notice. They have become "media events" whose comings and goings are featured in the gossip column rather than on the financial page. Economically, they have become irrelevant.

The power of the capitalists has gone down as fast as their economic importance. In 1907, J. P. Morgan's offer to buy shares was enough to stop a stock market panic. In 1922, one coal and steel magnate, Hugo Stinnes, single-handedly imposed on the German government the policy that pushed the country into hyperinflation. No businessman today would even dream of such action; he knows that he does not have the power. Expropriation and default have become infinitely more common in developing countries than they were in the late nineteenth and early twentieth centuries. But there is no more "gunboat diplomacy." In the 1970s it became an article of faith for the left—in Europe, in the United States, and especially in Latin America—that the U.S. government had conspired to overthrow the Allende regime in Chile to prevent the expropriation of the American-owned Chilean Telephone Company. The company did indeed try hard to get President Nixon to intervene—but without the slightest effect. When, in 1973, the Allende government was overthrown by a military coup, the U.S. government flatly refused to help the American company get back its property.

From the 1890s until World War II, business was the most powerful political lobby in Washington, even under "anti-business" administrations. After World War II the labor unions—which of course also are "business" in their concerns—became the most powerful pressure group in Washington (and in the capitals of all developed countries). Today it is the American Association of Retired People (AARP), whose 15 million members do indeed represent through their pension fund holdings the largest single block of ownership in America's industries. But they surely do not see themselves as "business," are not much concerned with issues affecting business, and share few, if any business values.

The Knowledge Worker and Business

A very large number of knowledge workers, perhaps the majority, will still be working in and for businesses. Yet their position is quite different from either that of yesterday's bosses or yesterday's workers. They are employees but at the same time are the only real capitalists through their pension funds. They do have a "boss" and are thus "subordinates." Many of them though have subordinates themselves and are themselves "bosses." Those who are still on the bottom rungs of the ladder certainly expect to be supervisors or department heads sooner or later. They are, moreover, specialists. Their own field may be quite narrow, but in it they know more than the boss—and they are aware of it. In their field they are superior to their employer no matter how low their standing in the organizational hierarchy. The knowledge worker is thus a colleague and an associate rather than a subordinate. He has to be managed as such.

One of Karl Marx's insights was that capital has mobility. In this it differs from all other "factors of production" such as land and labor. Capital can go where it is paid the most. Knowledge now has become the real capital of a developed economy. Knowledge workers know that their knowledge, even if not very advanced, gives them the freedom to move. In the tremendous reshuffling of American business during the 1980s, a great many displaced managers and professionals—even older people—found that they could get new jobs, and in many cases better jobs than the ones they had lost. Their knowledge made them free. It is a lesson knowledge people in America—and especially the young ones—have learned and will never forget. All of them—the geologist, the mathematician, the industrial engineer, the computer programmer, the secretary at the word processor, the personnel trainer, the accountant, the nurse, the salesperson—now know that they are not dependent on any one employer. Practically every institution needs them one way or another. Everyone's knowledge has a multitude of applications.

Increasingly, knowledge workers have two careers rather than one. Workers in the steel mill are ready to retire after thirty years of hard manual labor. After thirty years on the job knowledge workers are still fresh, physically and mentally; by then though they are bored. Most reached their terminal position long ago; their pension is vested and waiting for them when they reach sixty-five; the kids are grown up and the mortgage on the house is paid off. They are ready for a second career and may officially take early retirement. They may not take another paid job but—especially in the United States—go to work as volunteers for a non-profit institution. Some change what they are doing. Many more keep on doing the same work but in a different setting; the accountant, for instance, who moves from being controller of a small company to being controller in the local hospital or business manager of his local church. For all these people, the institution they work for is not primary; their knowledge, their craft is. That their employer is a business is not too important to them. In a year or two they might be working in a hospital or a local government agency or a consulting firm—or in another, different business. What is central to them in their work is the knowledge area, whether managing or petroleum engineering, working as an X-ray technician or as a tax analyst. Business is thus only the place where one works. "I work in a business but I am not a businessman; I am a market researcher," is what I hear again and again.

The New Career Options

In the nineteenth and early twentieth centuries, business was almost the only way out of grinding, hopeless poverty and lower-class status. There were far too few job opportunities in the professions and they were accessible, as a rule, only to the children of the affluent. In the developing countries this is still true. In the developed countries, however, the success of business has opened up a cornucopia of career options. Business is just one of them. Even in England, where the educational system has been a barrier to rather than a promoter of social mobility, education now offers the "lower classes" access to the job opportunities of the knowledge society.

Prior to the nineteenth century, there were almost no channels of social mobility. Son followed father behind the plow, most remaining hired hands all their lives. If a young woman did not have a dowry, she went into domestic service. The jobs in business which the nineteenth century created were the liberators. The young girl, perhaps not yet sixteen years old, in Theodore Dreiser's novel *Sister Carrie* (1900)— the most powerful picture of American society at the turn of the century—has no illusions as to what awaits her as a sewing-machine operator in a garment loft or a salesgirl in the merciless business metropolis of Chicago. Yet these jobs were her only chance to escape the hopelessness, drudgery, and crushing poverty of the hard-scrabble midwestern farm on which she had grown up. Work in the mill was still, twenty-five years later, the only way for another Dreiser heroine, the ill-starred Roberta of *An American Tragedy* (1925), to escape the same crushing, hopeless poverty of the farm.

The largest single occupational group in Britain in 1913

were domestic servants, mostly women. In 1914 the men went to war; women left domestic service and went into the munitions factories. Everybody knew that the day the war was over they would rush back from the "Satanic mills" into comfortable domestic service, where a "kind mistress" looked after them. Very, very few went back. No matter how hard the work in the factory, it was better—and much better paid—than being a maid. In the factory they worked fixed hours—and with World War I the eight-hour day was introduced—then they were through and on their own. In domestic service, they had to wait up until the mistress came home from a party at three o'clock in the morning.

There were not too many opportunities to rise into the middle class from a job in the factory or as a sales clerk. Those few were, however, the only opportunities that existed any place; a hired hand on the farm stayed a hired hand. Both Gottlieb Daimler, the German who in 1889 put the first motorcar on the market, and Henry Ford in the United States, started as workers. So did every single one of the early automobile manufacturers, and practically all other nineteenth-century manufacturers. Most of the bankers and great merchants of the century started out as penniless clerks. The resistance to, and contempt for, business and trade on the part of the upper classes—the English gentleman, the Prussian Junker, the French aristocrat, and the clergy—stemmed above all from resentment and fear of the social mobility business offered far too many members of the "lower orders," who then promptly forgot their "place."

The conditions under which the great majority of these workers and clerks lived were grim indeed: poor pay, long hours, back-breaking and unsafe work, rat-infested slum tenements. But for the millions who, like Dreiser's Sister Carrie and Roberta, streamed into business employment in the nineteenth-century cities, in Manchester, Glasgow, Boston, Chicago, Berlin, Vienna, Prague, Brussels, and Paris, business jobs, however grim, were still a big step up the ladder and the only one accessible to them.

But Sister Carrie's great-granddaughter—even if far less bright, ambitious, and gifted than Dreiser's heroine—would in the 1980s first graduate from the local high school and then go on to the state university with a nice scholarship. Four years later she would have too many choices. She might, of course, choose business, but she would start as a management trainee. If possessed of only half her great-grandmother's shrewdness and managerial talent, she would be an assistant vice president or a senior buyer within five years. The great-granddaughter might also go directly from college into the artistic career in which Sister Carrie ended up. She might become a radio announcer or teach music and acting at the high school she had graduated from. The granddaughter of Dreiser's Roberta—much less bright and ambitious than Carrie but warm and caring—could choose between becoming a nurse, a physical therapist, a kindergarten teacher, or the personnel manager in the plant where her grandmother had worked for starvation wages pushing a heavy needle through wet, stinking glove leather.

For people without college credentials, business employment as worker or clerk is still the best available job opportunity. And for the foreseeable future, business will remain the largest employer of the poorly schooled. But these business jobs no longer represent the opportunity they did a hundred years ago; they have become dead ends. Neither Gottlieb Daimler nor Henry Ford would have much of a chance now to get to the top without an engineering degree or an MBA. No reputable financial firm would be likely today to hire the "college dropout" J. P. Morgan. The jobs open to people without academic credentials are the same jobs that were open to such people a century ago. They are infinitely better paid, and in their working and living conditions they are (in developed countries) far superior to the conditions under which even privileged people worked and lived then. But such people are now the "losers," the ones who lack brains, ambition, and persistence. The "winners," the knowledge workers, are winners precisely because a business job is only one of their options. They are winners because they can choose.

Because they are knowledge workers, they are also not committed to any one employer or any kind of employing organization. It is immaterial to computer specialists whether they work for a department store, a university, a hospital, a government agency, or a stockbroker. What matters to them—other than the pay—is that the equipment is "state of the art" and the assignment challenging. That also goes for financial analyst and physical therapist; for personnel manager and metallurgist; for salesperson, graphic artist, and the assistant business manager of the local art gallery. These people are not anti-business; indeed, the term makes little sense to them. They may even "love" business, study management, and cherish the intellectual challenges that a business offers. But their first question is not likely to be: Is it good for the company, or for the hospital, or for the museum? It is more likely to be: Is it professional? To be sure, they know and by and large accept that the craft has to be adjusted to the mission, needs, and requirements of their employing institution. But that is increasingly a second rather than the first consideration; in fact, a great many knowledge workers, especially in businesses, see this as "top management's job" rather than "my job." Even in the large churches the "professionals"— the music director, or the heads of various "ministries" such as young people or young marrieds—tend to think of themselves first as musicians, youth workers, or marriage counselors, and only secondarily as pastors. This is right and proper, or at least inevitable. Knowledge workers will not do a good job unless they take their craft seriously.

In the value system of the knowledge worker, therefore, business values are subordinate and may even appear to be obstacles to performance. Even when knowledge workers are not a majority in their organization, they increasingly set the norms and standards. Indeed, one of the challenges ahead for any developed country—it is already very much an issue in the United States—is to maintain the commitment to economic performance that every developed country needs to remain competitive. How do we balance the knowledge worker's professional values with the need for traditional business values such as productivity and profitability in the economy and in the individual business?

These developments have gone furthest in the United States. In many other developed countries they are beginning. Only in Japan are they are still considered "unthinkable," especially by the older generation of corporate executives. But even in Japan they are inevitable, being implicit in the nature of knowledge. As knowledge becomes the central resource of the economy, society is bound to evolve into a post-business, knowledge society.

13

TWO COUNTERCULTURES

Knowledge workers are fast becoming the pacesetters in the societies of all developed countries. But the knowledge society also has its *countercultures*. The class that rose to dominance in the business society, the industrial worker, is becoming the "other half," representative of the 50 percent or so of the population who lack advanced schooling and with it access to knowledge jobs. And, though so far only in the United States, a second counterculture is emerging: the "third sector" of non-profit, non-governmental institutions. Their unpaid "volunteers" are the largest single group in the American workforce. And these third-sector organizations have a distinct ethos, distinct values, and make a distinct contribution. They are creating active and effective citizenship.

The Rise and Fall of the Blue-Collar Worker

No century before the twentieth experienced such rapid and radical social change. In developed countries, domestic servants have become virtually extinct; they had been a major social class in every society since the dawn of history. Farmers have become a small minority, even though in this century production on the farm has grown faster in the developed non-Communist countries than in any other sector. For millennia, farmers—whether agriculturalists or livestock growers—*were* civilization. The most dramatic event in this century's social history, however, has not been the decline of these ancient classes. It has been the rise and fall of the industrial worker.

When the early Socialists first identified the industrial worker as a new phenomenon, their forecasts of the rise of the proletariat—the 1848 *Communist Manifesto* by Karl Marx and Friedrich Engels, while most famous, is only one of them— was still more prophecy than diagnosis. By 1925, blue-collar workers in manufacturing industry had become the largest single occupational group, male or female. Twenty-five years later, in the 1950s, they and their unions had become the dominant political force in every non-Communist developed country. But in the early 1970s, industrial workers began to decline fast, first as a proportion of the workforce, then in numbers, and finally in political power and influence. Their decline has been even faster than their rise. By the year 2010—another twenty years on—they will have shrunk in the developed non-Communist countries to where farmers are now, that is, to between 5 and 10 percent of the workforce. It is by no means sure that their own institution, the labor union, can survive, and certain that it cannot survive in its traditional role and form.

Paradoxically the same force that underlay the meteoric rise of the industrial workers ultimately caused their fall: knowledge. For all nineteenth-century economists, including Marx, it was axiomatic that workers could only produce more by working harder or by working longer hours. It was an American engineer, Frederick W. Taylor, who did what no one had even thought of before: he treated manual work as something deserving study and analysis. Taylor showed that the real potential for increased output was to "work smarter." It was Taylor who defeated Marx and Marxism. Taylor's *Principles of Scientific Management* (1911) not only tremendously increased output. It made possible increasing workers' wages while at the same time cutting the product's prices and thereby increasing the demand for it. (Taylor actually refused to take a factory as a client unless the owners first substantially raised wages, sometimes tripling them.) Without Taylor, the number of industrial workers would still have grown fast, but they would have been Marx's exploited proletarians. Instead, the larger the number of blue-collar workers who went into the plants, the more they became "middle class" and "bourgeois" in their incomes and their standards of living. And the more they then turned conservative in their lifestyles and their values rather than becoming Marx's revolutionaries.

The next step in the use of knowledge—in full swing since 1970—applies analysis and system to the *productive process* itself. Its essence is not machinery (the term "automation" is quite misleading). General Motors found this out in the 1980s when it spent $30 billion on robots without much reduction in employment or costs or much improvement in quality. The essence of automated production is a system organized around information. But once that system has been designed, the need for manual work soon goes down dramatically. The center of gravity in production, and especially in manufacturing, then shifts from manual workers to knowledge workers. Far more middle-class jobs are being created by this process than old blue-collar jobs are being lost. Overall the process enriches as much as did the creation of well-paid blue-collar jobs in the last hundred years. We do not, in other words, face an economic problem, nor is there much danger of "alienation" or of creating a new "class war"—the old bugaboos of Marxist rhetoric. Even among the groups that are hardest hit by the shift—American blacks, steelworkers in England's Yorkshire, coal miners and steelworkers in the German

Ruhr— almost everyone has a brother, cousin, uncle, or aunt who got the needed schooling and has become a knowledge worker.

Nevertheless an extraordinary period has come to an end in which social advancement into affluence and middle-class status required only a union card rather than skill or knowledge. That a substantial and growing number of people with working-class backgrounds sit long enough in schools to become knowledge workers will only make things worse for those who don't. The less schooled will increasingly be seen by their more successful fellows, even by those who like educated American blacks are themselves members of a disadvantaged group, as failures, dropouts, as somehow "deficient," second-class citizens, "problems," and altogether inferior. The problem is not money. *It is dignity.*

In any society the people without education to qualify them for knowledge work will be a large group. In the United States, for instance, in the late eighties, only a quarter of those under age forty in the workforce had finished college. Another quarter had technical training beyond high school and were therefore also qualified for knowledge work, as nurses and legal secretaries, fashion buyers, graphic artists, computer technicians or dental hygienists and in a thousand or more knowledge-intensive pursuits. All these people have learned how to learn and so can use the opportunities for continuous learning that the American educational system offers. They enjoy substantial social status and significant promotional opportunities. But that still leaves half of the American labor force not qualified for knowledge work; the proportion is a good deal higher in Europe, and particularly high in Britain. There are plenty of non-knowledge jobs, more than we can easily fill, in fact. The problem is social status, recognition, self-respect. There is thus a real need to make non-knowledge jobs, many often requiring little skill, as productive and as self-respecting as possible. What is needed, above all, is to apply knowledge to such jobs as cleaning floors, making beds, or helping old, incapacitated people take care of themselves. Two large building-maintenance and home-maintenance companies, one Danish, one American, have built successful worldwide operations on endowing menial, unskilled work done by unschooled people with productivity, dignity, and opportunity. A few large American hospitals have done the same. These are beginnings only, but they do show that the job can be done. *And it needs to be done.*

The nineteenth century was convinced that the capitalist is capitalism's firstborn and favorite child. Most people still believe it. But economists have long known that it is untrue. Capitalists long antedated capitalism. The true children of the industrial economy were the industrial workers. They have been the modern economy's favorite children, and its main beneficiaries. It made them "middle class" in income, social status, and political power without their needing greater skill or greater knowledge while working far less hard and far less long than laborers ever did before. Now they are becoming the "other half"—but society cannot afford their becoming stepchildren.

Can the Labor Union Survive?

The labor union rose with the industrial worker; it was in fact the industrial worker's own institution. It is falling with the industrial worker. Can it survive at all?

The labor union might be judged this century's most successful institution. In 1900 it was still outlawed in most countries or barely tolerated. By 1920 it had become respectable. By the end of World War II, twenty-five years later, it had become dominant. Now the labor union is in tatters and disarray, apparently in irreversible decline. It is losing members fast; it is losing power even faster. As recently as 1974, the British Coal Miners Union could drive a Conservative government from power. Barely ten years later, Margaret Thatcher, successor to the Conservative Party leader whom the coal miners had defeated, broke the next miners' strike decisively and did so with overwhelming public support. Since then English trade unions have lost a quarter of their members. In the same period, labor unions in the United States have lost two fifths of their members. In the private sector they now enroll a lower proportion of workers—15 or 16 percent— than they did before the unionization drives during the late 1930s. When President Reagan dissolved the Air Traffic Controllers Union in the United States after it went on strike, he was overwhelmingly supported even by American union members. In Japan, the most powerful and most militant union could not prevent the privatization of the Japanese National Railways and has, as a result, been split from top to bottom. Union membership and union power are declining fast in Italy and France, and are beginning to do so in West Germany.

There are several explanations. The labor union certainly has much less to offer. Practically everything it stood for has become law in developed countries: short working hours, overtime pay, paid vacations, retirement pensions, and so on. The wage fund, that is, that part of the gross national product that goes to employees, now exceeds 80 or 85 percent in all developed countries. This means that there is no more "more" for union members. In most years the employee contribution to the employee's pension fund already exceeds by a good margin all the profit available to the shareholder.

There is also—the importance of this should not be underestimated—the steady deterioration in the quality of union leaders. Before World War II, rising into union leadership was the best opportunity for a young man from a working-class family. Now, ambitious young people go to the university, either full time or as evening students; four years later they are management trainees. Furthermore, the public perception of the labor union has gone down sharply. Instead of being the "protector of the weak" against "management power" and "management arrogance," it is seen increasingly as "arrogant" and "overpowering." The single most important factor in the decline of the labor union is however the shift in the center of gravity of the workforce from the blue-collar worker in manufacturing industry to the knowledge worker. Without the industrial workers' unions as its core, there is no labor movement.

We are so used to the labor union that we hardly notice how unique an institution it is. Management is a necessity in a society of organizations; but the labor union is not. Germany in 1933 had the largest, most respected, and apparently the strongest unions. Yet there was no resistance when Hitler suppressed them; and neither his grip on the country, nor industrial production, nor fighting morale in Nazi Germany were impaired by their absence.

The Choices

The labor union can go in one of three different directions. If it does nothing, it may disappear—even in a free, democratic society. Or it may shrink to the point where it becomes irrelevant. This seems to be the direction in which the British, Italian, and French unions are moving, but also most of those in the United States.

A second choice is to try to maintain itself by dominating the political power structure, having government impose compulsory union membership and such power positions for the union as "co-determination," which gives it a veto power over company management. This may appear a rational course; the unions in Germany, Holland, and Scandinavia seem to have chosen it. After all, the feudal knights and their descendants maintained themselves this way in power and privilege for five hundred years, even though they had lost all social function by the year 1400. But then the feudal knights had a monopoly on arms and with it overwhelming military power. The equivalent in today's society would be over-whelming voting power—and that the labor union has already lost.

There is a third choice: that the union rethink its function. The union might reinvent itself as the organ of society—and of the employing institution—concerned with human poten-tial and human achievement, and with optimizing the human resource altogether. The union would still have a role as the representative of the employees against management stupid-ity, management arbitrariness, and management abuse of power. This would not be an adversarial relationship, but would resemble that of the Scandinavian Ombudsman. The union would work with management on productivity and quality, on keeping the enterprise competitive, and thus maintaining the members' jobs and their incomes.

Such a role may sound utopian, but it is pretty much the way the Japanese labor union functions—made possible, of course, because of the Japanese employer's commitment to the job security of "lifetime employment." Amazingly enough, the United Automobile Workers Union (UAW), still one of the most militant of American industrial unions, has begun to move—slowly and against heavy internal resis-tance—toward such a radical redefinition of its policies, be-havior, and position. Both General Motors and Ford now have joint management–union committees to reduce union work rules, a main cause of both America's high costs and poor quality, and to boost productivity and quality. To be sure, this required promises on the part of the companies of job security for union members. And it would not have hap-pened at all if Japanese automobile manufacturers—Toyota, Nissan, Honda, Mazda—had not built plants in the United States that have either no union at all or union contracts without job restrictions and work rules. The UAW therefore had little choice—and a few good years of GM and Ford may well lure it back to its old self-defeating policies. Another

American union is also rethinking its role and function. The local school boards in the United States fear and loathe the American Federation of Teachers, with its "outrageous" demands for higher teacher salaries and teacher control of the schools. Yet this militant union also demands that teachers be held accountable for the learning performance of pupils, that they be paid accordingly, and that non-performing teachers be dismissed rather than protected by tenure.

These are but straws in the wind, and so far it is not a strong wind. But can the labor union—whether of manual, clerical, or knowledge workers—survive at all unless it accepts as an opportunity the shift to the world economy and to the knowledge society?

Citizenship Through the Third Sector

The counterculture of the "other half" in the knowledge society is one of social status and lifestyles. The other—so far purely American—counterculture is one of values. It is the counterculture of the non-business, non-government, "human-change agencies," the non-profit organizations of the so-called third sector.

In the 1950s the United States seemed totally out of step with the rest of the non-Communist developed world. It was capitalist and free enterprise whereas everybody else was marching toward socialism and a planned economy. Thirty-five years later everybody else has become as capitalist as the United States ever was—and even the Communist countries are talking "private enterprise," "stock markets," "productivity," and "profits." In many areas the United States today may even be a good deal more statist and less open to "free enterprise" than many other non-Communist, developed countries—in product liability, for instance, in the approval process for new drugs, in environmental restrictions, or in the regulations of banking and finance.

At the same time, U.S. society has become different and

distinct from other countries—developed or developing, free market or socialist—in the steady growth of its third sector, the thousands of non-profit but non-governmental institutions. These institutions include the majority of America's hospitals, a very large part of the schools, and an even larger percentage of colleges and universities. They include large international philanthropic organizations and very large domestic ones like the American Red Cross with its thousands of local chapters and a million volunteers nationwide. They include many purely local ones, e.g., the community chests which support local charities in every American city and county, or the thousands of "Meals on Wheels" whose volunteers take hot lunches to the sick and elderly. They include large national health-care groups such as the American Heart Association, the American Lung Association, the American Mental Health Association. They include a great many community service groups: the Salvation Army, the Girl Scouts (which now enroll one out of every four American girls of elementary school age), the Boy Scouts, or the Urban League, the effective community service of America's black city dwellers. They include the enormous diversity of churches in the United States ranging from those with more than ten thousand parishioners to conventicles with twenty-five members. And they include an indescribable variety of cultural enterprises—hundreds of symphony orchestras, for instance, and any number of museums. These institutions are paid mainly by fees and voluntary donations rather than by tax dollars. They are independent and governed by their own volunteer boards. But even a good many tax-supported and governmental activities in the United States are run like third-sector institutions, the public school, for instance, or the state universities and community colleges. In Europe or Japan such institutions are largely controlled and run by a central government. In the United States they are mostly run autonomously, though paid for by government and out of tax money.

They have their own budget and are run by administrators chosen by a locally elected board.

Third-sector institutions are not unknown in other countries. They occupy the "commanding heights" in Britain's education—what with the prep schools, the public schools, and the two prestige universities of Oxford and Cambridge. In Britain there are also the Non-conformist churches. In Japan there are private universities and private non-governmental hospitals, many of them originally founded by Christian missionaries. The missionaries also gave Korea independent churches and schools affiliated with them. But few such institutions exist on the European continent. And even in Britain, Japan, and Korea, they are confined to a few tasks. In the United States they are ubiquitous. They fulfill a unique social function. They are a counterculture, different and separate from both the governmental and the business sectors and their respective values and cultures.

The third sector is actually the country's largest employer, though neither its workforce nor the output it produces show up in the statistics. One out of every two adult Americans—a total of 90 million people—are estimated to work as volunteers in the third sector, most of them in addition to holding a paid job. These volunteers put in the equivalent of 7.5 million *full-time* work years. If they were paid, their wages would amount to $150 billion a year; but of course they are not paid. The third sector largely explains why taxes in the United States are lower than in Europe. Spending on public and community purposes is actually quite a bit higher in the United States, but a substantial portion, as much as 15 percent of GNP, does not flow through tax channels. It goes directly, as fees, as insurance premiums, as charitable contributions, and as unpaid work, to non-governmental third-sector institutions.

Yet few people realize the size, let alone the importance, of the third sector. In fact, few people are even aware of its existence. People do know, of course, of the churches—most people in the United States are still church members. They do know of the hospital, the YMCA, the Scouts, the United Way, the local museum. But few people see these institutions as having anything in common except that they all ask for money. Until very recently even the third-sector institutions shared the laity's perception that churches were one thing, hospitals another, and the Scouts yet something else. This has changed; the institutions do know now that they discharge a common function, even though each of the individual units has a separate and distinct mission.

These institutions, today, increasingly talk of the "independent sector" rather than the "third sector." But even that term begs the question what the *function* is that these institutions perform. The definition most commonly used is that they are neither "government" nor "business." This is misleading, however. Only for the tax collector does it make a difference that a given hospital is "non-profit" and purely local, a unit in a non-profit chain such as many Catholic and Lutheran hospitals in the United States, or a unit of a business such as Hospital Corporation of America or Humana. In the way the hospital is run, in its behavior, its activities, and its values, there is nothing to tell the one from the other. The people serving in such a hospital often do not know whether their employer is non-profit or for profit. And frequently neither the professor nor the student cares whether a given college or university is "private" or "state."

Non-profit, non-business, non-governmental are all negatives. One cannot, however, define anything by what it is not. What, then, is it that all these institutions *do*? They all have in common—and this is a recent realization—that their purpose is to change human beings. The product of the hospital is a cured patient. The product of a church is a changed life. The product of the Salvation Army—the one organization that reaches the poorest of the poor regardless of race or religion—is a derelict become a citizen. The product of the Girl Scouts is a mature young woman who has values, skills, and respect for herself. The purpose of the Red Cross in peacetime is to enable a community hit by natural disaster to regain its capacity to look after itself, to create human competence. The product of the American Heart Association are middle-aged people who look after their own health and practice preventative cardiac maintenance in the way they live, the way they eat, the way they do not smoke, cut back on their drinking, exercise, and so on.

"Human-change institutions" would be the right name. Every developed country discharges most of these functions. But in most of such countries they are discharged through a governmental, centralized agency. What makes the United States distinct is that these functions are being discharged in and by the local community and, in the great majority of cases, by autonomous, self-governing, local organizations.

The Growth of the Third Sector

That the tasks the human-change institutions perform is organized differently in the United States is only one of the third sector's important characteristics. The third sector has also grown fast, especially in the last ten or fifteen years. Indeed, during the eighties it has been the fastest-growing part of American society. And equally noteworthy is the way this growth has come about: it is growth in effectiveness as much as it is growth in size.

Here are a few examples, picked at random. A church-related health-care chain, owning a dozen large hospitals and a dozen nursing homes, has increased its income by a third in the last ten years during which most American hospitals suffered sharp income drops. Where most hospitals are running deficits, this chain breaks even. At the same time the chain's hospitals are steadily improving their performance, both in medical care and in patient care. The Girl Scouts of

199

the U.S.A., the world's largest women's organization, has managed to maintain its membership at 3.5 million despite a drop of almost one fifth in the number of girls of school age between 1978 and 1988, thus significantly increasing its market penetration. In the state of Florida, criminals who are sentenced to jail for the first time—there are about 25,000 of them at any one time—are now paroled into the custody of the Salvation Army. These convicts are poor risks, being mostly poor blacks or Hispanics with two or three previous arrests. Three out of every four of them would become habitual criminals if actually sent to jail. The Salvation Army, however, rehabilitates three out of four of the parolees.

Not all third-sector institutions are doing well; the third sector too has its "Rust Belt." Church membership and attendance have been going down quite sharply in all denominations, whether "liberal," "mainstream," "evangelical," or "fundamentalist." But membership and attendance are growing fast in "pastoral" churches—Protestant and Catholic, "mainstream" and "evangelical"—which concentrate on serving the parishioners, their needs, their problems, their families. Around 1970 there were no more than five thousand pastoral churches with a membership of two thousand parishioners or more. By the late eighties their number had grown fourfold, to twenty thousand. And they alone employ probably more than a million volunteers as unpaid staff.

Americans do not give a larger share of their income in voluntary donations than they have done for many years. Larger revenues do not, therefore, explain the third-sector successes. They are based on greatly increased productivity. Third-sector institutions—or at least a large number of them—get more results out of the same resources. The growth of the third sector is primarily a management achievement.

The Catholic hospital group mentioned earlier practices what every management text preaches. It treats change as opportunity. It aggressively pushes innovations: free-standing surgical and ophthalmological units, free-standing rehabilitation centers. It is by no means alone in running its own Health Maintenance Organization (HMO) in every city where it has a hospital. But instead of using the HMO to fight a problem, that is, to fill beds in half-empty hospitals, it runs the HMO to make money by keeping the largest possible number of patients out of the hospital.

The Girl Scouts of the U.S.A. saw their opportunity in demographic change. They adapted their programs and activities to the married woman with children who is now in the labor force. Recognizing that the career aspirations of girls are changing fast in America, they converted those changes into opportunities. They began to recruit aggressively among minorities, the blacks, the Hispanics, the Asians, offering both minority children and their mothers participation in what had up to then been considered a white, middle-class activity. Fifteen years ago the Girl Scouts were preponderantly white. By 1987 the proportion of black girls of elementary school age enrolled in the Girl Scouts matched that of white girls.

Since it was first founded one hundred twenty-five years ago, the Salvation Army has worked in the slums of big cities to keep endangered young people out of a life of crime—with minimal success. What the Salvation Army used was a "management tool": organized abandonment. It asked, "If we were not already doing crime prevention in the slums, would we now, knowing what we know, go into it?" The moment the Salvation Army asked this question, it realized that the answer was no. The "return on the investment"—a substantial investment of time and effort by large numbers of Salvation Army people—was close to zero. Once the question was asked, it became clear why the program had been unsuccessful. Before being caught and convicted, endangered young people in the slums are not receptive to the Salvation Army's message. Each of them thinks, "I'll beat the odds," and being arrested but released on probation only confirms this belief. After young people have served even a short term in jail, it is too late. They are traumatized by their experience and corrupted by it. For a very short period there is a "target of opportunity": pre-convicts, the ones who have been caught and sentenced to jail but have not yet served there. They are sufficiently frightened but not yet corrupted.

The success of the pastoral churches is a marketing success. They asked, Who are our customers and what is of value to them? They saw in the fact that the young educated people do not go to church an opportunity.

In every case what was done could have been learned from any management text. That opportunities must not be subordinated to problems—the key to the hospital group's success—is axiomatic (see, for instance, my book *Innovation and Entrepreneurship*, 1985). All that the Girl Scouts did was to look at the demographics. The Salvation Army applied organized abandonment. The pastoral churches did what every text on marketing prescribes: they researched the people who should be customers but aren't.

The successful and growing non-profit third-sector organizations also apply management internally. They work on making their governing boards effective. A good many of them now routinely ask a potential board member, "What contribution should we hold you accountable for should you join our board?" "What specific work are you going to perform?" They have work programs against which they regularly evaluate their boards. They practice management by objectives, and more thoroughly than most businesses do. Staff members, whether paid or unpaid, are expected—in the Girl Scouts or the Salvation Army—to define clearly the performance and contribution for which they are to be held accountable. They are then regularly appraised against these performance objectives. Staff members—paid or unpaid—

who do not perform are no longer kept on; they are either moved to assignments in which they can perform, or they are eased out, compassionately but firmly. To make this possible, the third-sector institutions have gone heavily into training. A good many of them now routinely put all their people, from the chief executive officer to the newest volunteer, into training sessions in which everyone acts both as a trainer in one area and a student in all the others. More and more of the third-sector institutions are shifting their focus from the "good cause" to performance and accountability.

No More "Volunteers"

In the well-run third-sector organization, there are no more "volunteers." There is only unpaid staff. A large pastoral church runs a dozen ministries, both for its thirteen thousand members and in its community. Yet it has a paid staff of only one hundred sixty. New members of the congregation are asked after a few months to become "unpaid staff," are thoroughly trained, and given a specific assignment with performance goals. Their performance is regularly reviewed. If it does not come up to high expectations, the volunteer is either shifted to another, less demanding assignment or asked to resign. The Salvation Army keeps a tight rein on its 25,000 parolees in Florida. But only one hundred sixty paid staffers are assigned to the task; they supervise and train volunteers and take care of crises. The work itself is done by two hundred fifty to three hundred unpaid people. What enabled the Girl Scouts to maintain enrollment in a shrinking market was a substantial increase in the number of volunteers: from 600,-000 to 730,000. Many of the new volunteers are young professional women without children of their own—at least so far—but with a need to be a woman in a feminine environment a few evenings a week and on weekends, and to be with children. They are attracted precisely because the job is professional; they are required to spend several hours a week being trained or as trainers for newcomers. In fact, the unpaid staff is taking more and more of the work formerly done by paid professionals in third-sector organizations.

No organization more carefully guards the professional's privileges than the Catholic Church guards those of its priests. As the number of priests in the Catholic Church in America goes down—and it has been doing so fast—a diocese should thus be expected to retrench. But one midwestern diocese has doubled its community services even though it has barely half the number of priests it had twenty years ago. Its one hundred forty priests preach, say mass, hear confession, baptize, confirm, marry, and bury people. Everything else is done by two thousand lay people, each expected to work at least three hours a week and to spend an additional two or three hours in training sessions. Each lay person's performance is appraised twice a year against performance objectives. "It's worse than Marine boot camp," one of these unpaid staffers says. Yet there is a long waiting list of potential volunteers.

The third-sector institutions, in sum, not only practice management, in some cases more seriously than American businesses. They are becoming management innovators and management pioneers.

The Third Sector as Counterculture

America's third-sector institutions are rapidly becoming creators of new bonds of community and a bridge across the widening gap between knowledge workers and the "other half." Increasingly they create a sphere of effective citizenship. One hears a good deal these days about the disintegration of community; the family, for instance, or the community of the small town. Traditional communities in all developed countries are weakening, except perhaps in Japan. But in the third-sector institution new bonds of community are being forged. In volunteer work retired working-class people and young knowledge workers work together—in the Salvation Army's work with young convicts, say, or in designing programs and training leaders in a local chapter of the American Mental Health Association. What the Girl Scouts contribute to black women in the inner city may be more important than what they contribute to black children. These women are becoming leaders in their community, learning skills, setting examples, gaining recognition and status. Indeed, there are now more blacks in leadership positions in the two U.S. scouting organizations—the Boy Scouts and the Girl Scouts—than anywhere else except in black churches. And in the Scouts they are leaders in racially integrated organizations, that is, in American society rather than in a segregated society.

Even more important may be the role of the third-sector institution in creating for its volunteers a sphere of meaningful citizenship. Now that the size and complexity of government make direct participation all but impossible, it is the human-change institution of the third sector that is offering its volunteers a sphere of personal achievement in which the individual exercises influence, discharges responsibility, and makes decisions. And increasingly executives in business, especially people in middle management, are expected to serve in decision-making positions as board members of non-profit institutions. In the political culture of mainstream society, individuals, no matter how well educated, how successful, how achieving, or how wealthy, can only vote and pay taxes. They can only react, can only be passive. In the counterculture of the third sector, they are active citizens. This may be the most important contribution of the third sector. So far it is a purely American achievement.

In its American form, the third-sector institution can only flourish in American soil. No other country has the tradition of the frontier with its isolated communities forced to work together and to be self-sufficient, combined with the pluralism of self-governing churches, independent of state and government and therefore dependent on their congregations. No European culture, not even the closely knit Latin family, could nurture this kind of community. Only the radically different history of Japan has bequeathed a tradition of community that is comparable—in the "family" of the employing institution which translates the bonds of the feudal clan, the *han,* into the modern institution of government agency or business enterprise.

And still the knowledge society—with a social mobility that threatens to become rootlessness, with its "other half," its dissolution of the ties of farm and small town and their narrow horizons—needs community, freely chosen yet acting as a bond. It needs a sphere where the individual can become a master through serving. It needs a sphere where freedom is not just being passive, not just being left alone rather than being ordered around—a sphere that requires active involvement and responsibility.

14

THE INFORMATION-BASED

ORGANIZATION

The typical large organization, such as a large business or a government agency, twenty years hence will have no more than half the levels of management of its counterpart today, and no more than a third the number of "managers." In its structure, and in its management problems and concerns, it will bear little resemblance to the typical manufacturing company, circa 1950, which our textbooks still consider the norm. Instead, it is far more likely to resemble organizations that neither the practicing manager nor the student of management and administration pays much attention to today: the hospital, the university, the symphony orchestra. For, like them, the business, and increasingly the government agency as well, will be knowledge-based, composed largely of specialists who direct and discipline their own performance through organized feedback from colleagues and customers. It will be an information-based organization.

Large organizations will have little choice but to become information-based. Demographics, for one, demands the shift. The center of gravity in employment is moving fast from manual and clerical workers to knowledge workers who resist the command-and-control model that business took from the military one hundred years ago. Economics also dictates change, especially the need for large businesses to innovate and to be entrepreneurs. But above all, information technology demands the shift.

An information-based organization can be built without advanced data-processing technology. As we shall see, the British built just such an organization in India when "information technology" meant the quill pen, and barefoot runners were "telecommunications." But as advanced technology becomes more and more prevalent, organizations have to engage in analysis and diagnosis—that is, in information. Otherwise, they will be swamped by the data they generate. So far, most computer users still use the new technology to do faster what they have always done before—"crunch" conventional numbers. As soon, however, as an organization takes the first tentative steps from data to information, its decision processes, management structure, and the way its work gets done begin to be transformed. This process is already moving fast throughout the world, and especially in the large transnational companies.

Consider the impact of computer technology on capital-investment decisions. We have known for a long time that there is no one right way to analyze a proposed capital investment. To understand it, we need at least six pieces of information: the expected rate of return; the payout and the investment's expected productive life; the discounted present value of all returns through the productive lifetime of the investment; the risk in not making the investment or deferring it; the cost and risk in case of failure; and finally the opportunity cost that is the return from alternative investments. Every accounting student is taught these concepts. But before the advent of data-processing capacity, the actual analyses would have taken man-years of clerical toil to complete. Now anyone with a spreadsheet should be able to do them in a few hours. The availability of information thus transforms the capital-investment analysis from opinion into diagnosis, that is, into the rational weighing of alternative assumptions. Information transforms the capital-investment decision from an opportunistic, financial decision, governed by the numbers, into a business decision based on the probability of alternative strategic assumptions. As a result, the decision both presupposes a business strategy and challenges that strategy and its assumptions. What was once a budget exercise becomes an analysis of policy.

The second area that is affected when an organization focuses its data-processing capacity on producing information is its structure. Almost immediately, it becomes clear that both the number of management levels and the number of managers can be sharply cut. It turns out that whole layers of management neither make decisions nor lead. Instead, their main, if not their only, function is to serve as "relays"—human boosters for the faint, unfocused signals that pass for communication in the traditional pre-information organization. One of America's largest defense contractors made this discovery when it asked what information its top corporate and operating managers needed to do their jobs. Where did it come from? What form was it in? How did it flow? The search for answers soon revealed that whole layers of management—perhaps as many as six out of a total of fourteen—existed only because these questions had not been asked before. The company had had data galore; but it had always used its copious data for control rather than for information.

Information is data endowed with relevance and purpose. Converting data into information thus requires knowledge. And knowledge, by definition, is specialized. (In fact, truly knowledgeable people tend toward overspecialization because there is always so much more to know.) The information-based organization requires far more specialists overall than does the command-and-control structure we are accustomed to. Moreover, the specialists work in operations rather than at corporate headquarters. The operating organization becomes an organization of specialists of all kinds. Information-based organizations need central operating work such as legal counsel, public relations, human resources, and labor relations as much as ever. But the need for service staffs—that is, for people without operating responsibilities who advise, counsel, or coordinate—shrinks drastically. In its *central* management, the information-based organization needs few, if any, specialists.

Because of its flatter structure, the large, information-based organization will more closely resemble the organization of one hundred and fifty years ago than today's big companies or big government agencies. Back then, however, all the knowledge, such as it was, resided in the very top people. There was the minister in a government agency and his secretary. In a business, even a large one, there were a few partners and department heads. The rest were helpers or hands, who mostly performed the same work and did as they were told. In the information-based organization, knowledge will lie primarily at the bottom, in the minds of the specialists who do different work and direct themselves. Today's typical organization, in which knowledge tends to be concentrated in service staffs perched rather insecurely between top management and the operating people, will likely be labeled a phase, an attempt to infuse knowledge from the top rather than obtain information from below.

A good deal of the work will be done differently in the information-based organization as a result. Traditional departments will serve as guardians of standards, as centers for training and for the assignment of specialists. The work itself will largely be done by task-focused teams. This change is already under way in what used to be the most clearly defined of all areas in a business: research. In pharmaceuticals, in telecommunications, in papermaking, the traditional sequence of research, development, manufacturing, and marketing is being replaced by *synchrony:* specialists from all these functions work together as a team, from the inception of research to a product's establishment in the market. And this is likely to become the model generally for the performance of knowledge work. We already see in the university the emergence of interdisciplinary teams. Even in the military, the traditional fixed command structure, though an absolute necessity under combat conditions, is being supplemented by ad hoc task forces for special assignments.

Yet the assignment of a task force, its composition, and its leadership will have to be decided on case by case. The organization that will be developed will, therefore, go beyond the matrix and may be quite different from it. One thing is clear, though: the information-based organization requires self-discipline and an emphasis on individual responsibility for relationships and for communications.

Some Earlier Examples

It is too early perhaps to draw an organization chart of the information-based organization of tomorrow. But there are clues in other kinds of information-based organizations, such as the hospital, the symphony orchestra, and the earlier British administration in India.

A fair-sized American hospital of about four hundred beds has several hundred attending physicians and a staff of twelve to fifteen hundred paramedics divided among some sixty medical and paramedical specialties. Each specialty has its own knowledge, its own training, its own language. In each specialty, particularly the paramedical ones like the clinical lab and physical therapy, the head person is a working specialist rather than a full-time manager. The head of each specialty reports directly to the top and there is little middle management. A good deal of the work is done in ad hoc teams as required by an individual patient's diagnosis and condition.

A large symphony orchestra is even more instructive. In some modern symphonies, hundreds of musicians are on stage together and play together. According to organization theory, there should be several "group vice president conductors" and perhaps a half-dozen "division VP conductors." But there is only one conductor—and every one of the musicians, each a high-grade specialist, plays directly to that person, without an intermediary.

Perhaps the best example of a large and successful information-based organization, and one without any middle management at all, was the British-run civil service in India. The British ran the Indian subcontinent for two hundred years, from the middle of the eighteenth century through World War II, without making fundamental changes in organization structure or administrative policy. The Indian Civil Service never had more than one thousand members to administer a vast and densely populated subcontinent—a tiny fraction (at most 1 percent) of the legions of Confucian mandarins and palace eunuchs employed to administer a not-much-more populous China (and an even tinier fraction of the 22 million civil servants an independent India now employs). Most of the Britishers were quite young; a thirty-year-old was a survivor, especially in the early years. Most lived alone in isolated outposts with the nearest countryman a day or two of travel away. And for the first hundred years there was neither telegraph nor railroad.

The organization structure was totally flat. Each district officer reported directly to the "Chief Operating Officer," the provincial Political Secretary. Since there were nine provinces, each Political Secretary had about one hundred people reporting directly to him, many times what the doctrine of span of control would allow. Nevertheless, the system worked remarkably well for a long time, in large part because it was designed to ensure that each of its members had the information he needed to do his job. Each month the district officer spent a whole day writing a full report to the Political Secretary in the provincial capital. He discussed his principal tasks—there were only four, each clearly delineated: prevent the natives from killing each other in racial and religious conflicts; keep down banditry; dispense justice impartially and honestly; assess and collect taxes. He put down in detail what he had expected would happen with respect to each of these tasks, what actually did happen, and why the two differed if there was a discrepancy. Then he wrote down what he expected would happen in the ensuing month with respect to each key task and what he was going to do about it, asked questions about policy, and commented on long-term opportunities, threats, and needs. In turn, the Political Secretary "minuted" every one of those reports, writing back a full commentary.

What Are the Requirements?

On the basis of these examples, what can we say about the requirements of the information-based organization? And what are its management problems likely to be?

Several hundred musicians and their conductor can play together because they all have the same score. It tells flutist, timpanist, and conductor what to play, who is to play it, and when it is to be played. The specialists in the hospital all share a common mission: the care and cure of the sick. The diagnosis is their "score"; it dictates specific actions for the X-ray lab, the dietician, the physical therapist, and the rest of the hospital team. Information-based organizations, in other words, require clear, simple, common objectives that translate into particular actions. At the same time, as these examples indicate, information-based organizations also need concentration on one objective or, at most, on a few.

Because the "players" in an information-based organization are specialists, they cannot be told how to do their work.

213

There are probably few orchestra conductors who could coax even one note out of a French horn, let alone show the horn player how to do it. But the conductor knows how to focus the horn player's skill and knowledge on the orchestra's joint performance. This focus is the model for the leader of an information-based organization. Yet neither business nor government agency has a "score" to play by. The score is written as it plays. Neither a first-rate performance of a symphony nor a miserable one will change what the composer wrote. But the performance of a business, a government agency, or a military service continually creates new and different scores against which its performance is assessed. An information-based organization must therefore be structured around goals that clearly state management's performance expectations for the enterprise and for each part and specialist. It must be organized around feedback that compares results and expectations so that every member can exercise self-control.

Another requirement of the information-based organization is that everyone take information responsibility. The bassoonist in the orchestra does so every time she plays a note. Doctors and paramedics work with an elaborate system of reports centered in the nurse's station on the patient's floor. The district officer in India lived up to this responsibility every time he filed a report. The key to such a system is that everyone asks: Who in this organization depends on me for what information? And on whom, in turn, do I depend? The list will always include superiors and subordinates. The most important names, however, will be those of *colleagues,* people with whom one's primary relationship is coordination. The relationship between internist, surgeon, and anesthesiologist is one example. But the relationship of biochemist, pharmacologist, medical director in charge of clinical testing, and marketing specialist in a pharmaceutical company is no different. It, too, requires each person to take the fullest information responsibility.

Information responsibility to others is increasingly understood, especially in middle-sized companies. But information responsibility to oneself is still largely neglected. Everyone in the information-based organization needs constantly to be thinking through what information he or she requires to do the job and make a contribution. This may well be the most radical break with the way even the most highly computerized businesses are still being run today. There, people either assume that the more data they get, the more information they have—which was a perfectly valid assumption yesterday when data were scarce; now that data are plentiful, however, it leads only to data overload and information blackout. Or they believe that the information specialists know what data executives and professionals need in order to have information. But information specialists are toolmakers. They can tell us what tool to use to hammer upholstery nails into a chair; we need to decide whether we should be upholstering a chair at all.

Executives and professional specialists therefore have to think through what is information for them, that is, what data they need: first, to know what they are doing; then, to be able to decide what they should be doing; and finally, to appraise how well they are doing. Until this happens, the now popular Management Information Systems Departments are likely to remain cost centers rather than becoming the result centers they could be.

Government agencies, businesses, labor unions, the military—even large school districts and large Catholic dioceses—will thus have to change old habits and acquire new ones. The more successful an organization has been, the more difficult and painful this process is apt to be. It threatens

215

the jobs, the status, and the opportunities of a good many people, especially the long-serving, middle-aged people in middle management who tend to be the least mobile and who feel most settled in their work, their positions, their relationships, and their behavior.

The Problems

The information-based organization poses new management problems. I see as particularly critical:

- Developing rewards, recognition, and career opportunities for specialists;
- Creating unified vision in an organization of specialists;
- Devising the management structure for an organization of task forces;
- Ensuring the supply, preparation, and testing of top management people.

Bassoonists as a rule neither want nor expect to be anything but bassoonists. Their career opportunities consist in moving from second to first bassoon and perhaps in moving from a second-rank orchestra to a better-paying and more prestigious one. Similarly, medical technologists neither expect nor want to be anything but medical technologists. Their career opportunities consist of a fairly good chance of moving up to senior technician, and a slim chance of becoming lab director. For those who make it to lab director—about one out of every twenty-five or thirty technicians—there is also the opportunity to move to a bigger, richer hospital. The district officer in India had practically no career opportunities except to be moved to a different district after a three-year stint. Opportunities for specialists in an information-based business organization should be more plentiful than they are in an orchestra or hospital, let alone in the Indian Civil Service. But, as in these organizations, they will primarily be opportunities for advancement within the specialty, and for limited advancement at that. Advancement into management will be the exception, for the simple reason that there will be far fewer middle management positions to move into. This new reality contrasts sharply with the traditional organization where, except in the research lab, the main line of advancement has been to move out of the specialty and into general management.

More than thirty years ago the (American) General Electric Company tackled this problem by creating "parallel opportunities" for "individual professional contributors." Many companies have followed this example. Professional specialists however have largely rejected it as a solution. They—and their management colleagues—generally view promotions into management as the only meaningful opportunities. The prevailing compensation structure in practically all large organizations reinforces this attitude. It is heavily biased toward managerial positions and titles—even in a Catholic diocese, let alone in a business, a government agency, or a military service. There are no easy solutions to this dilemma. Some help may come from looking at large law firms and consulting firms, where even the most senior partner tends to be a specialist, and where associates who will not make partner are "outplaced" fairly early. Whatever is developed eventually will work only if the compensation structures of large organizations are drastically changed.

The second challenge that management faces is giving an organization of specialists a common vision, a view of the whole. In the Indian Civil Service, the district officer was expected to see the "whole" of his district. To enable him to concentrate on the "big picture," the government services that arose one after the other in the nineteenth century (forestry, irrigation, the archeological survey, public health and sanitation, roads) were organized *outside* the administrative structure and had virtually no contact with the district officer. This however increasingly isolated the district officer from the activities that often had the greatest impact on—and the greatest importance for—his district. In the end, only the provincial government or the central government in Delhi had a view of the "whole," and it was an increasingly abstract one at that.

A business, a government agency, a hospital, cannot function this way. It requires that the view of the whole and a focus on the whole be shared among a great many professional specialists, certainly among the senior ones. Yet it will have to accept, and even foster, the pride and professionalism of its specialists—if only because their motivation must come from that pride and professionalism in the absence of opportunities to move into middle management. One way to provide a view of the whole, of course, is through work in cross-functional task forces. The information-based organization will use more and smaller self-governing units, assigning them tasks tidy enough for "a good man to get his arms around," as the old phrase has it. But to what extent should information-based organizations rotate performing specialists out of their specialties and into new ones? And to what extent will top management have to accept as a top priority making and maintaining common vision across professional specialties?

Heavy reliance on task-force teams assuages one problem. But it aggravates another: the management structure of the information-based organization. Who will the managers be? Will they be task-force leaders? Or will there be a two-headed monster—one a specialist structure, comparable perhaps to the way attending physicians function in a hospital; another an administrative structure of task-force leaders? The decisions we face on the role and function of the task-force leaders are risky and controversial. Is theirs a permanent assignment, analogous to the job of the supervisory nurse in the hospital? Or is it a function of the task that changes as the task does? Is it an assignment or a position? Does it carry any rank at all?

And if it does, will the task-force leaders become in time what the product managers have been in a typical large consumer-goods company, or at an advertising agency: the basic units of management and the organization's field officers? Might the task-force leaders eventually replace department heads and vice presidents?

Already there are signs of every one of these developments. But there is neither a clear trend nor much understanding as to what each entails. Certainly each would give rise to a different organizational structure from any we are familiar with.

Where Will Top Management Come From?

The toughest problem will be the supply, preparation, and testing of top management people. This is, of course, an old and central dilemma, as well as a major reason for the general acceptance of decentralization in large businesses in the last forty years. Existing organizations have a great many middle management positions that are supposed to prepare and test a person. As a result, there are usually a good many people to choose from when filling a senior management slot. When the number of middle management positions is sharply cut, where will the information-based organization's top executives come from? What will be their preparation? How will they have been tested?

Decentralization into autonomous units will surely be even more critical than it is now. Large businesses may copy the German *Gruppe,* in which the decentralized units are set up as separate companies with their own top managements. The Germans use this model precisely because of their tradition of promoting people in their specialties, especially in research and engineering. If they could not put people into commands in near-independent subsidiaries, they would have little opportunity to train and test their most promising professionals.

These subsidiaries are thus somewhat like the farm teams of an American major-league baseball club.

We may also find that more and more top management jobs in big companies will be filled by hiring people away from smaller companies. This is the way that major orchestras get their conductors: young conductors earn their spurs in a small orchestra or opera house, only to be hired away by a larger one. The heads of a large hospital often have had similar careers.

Can business follow the example of orchestra and hospital where top management has become a separate career? Conductors and hospital administrators come respectively out of courses in conducting and schools of hospital administration. In France, large companies are often run by men who have spent their entire previous career in government service. But in most countries this would be unacceptable to the organization (only France has the mystique of the *grandes écoles*). And even in France, businesses, especially large ones, are becoming too demanding to be run by people without firsthand experience and a proven success record. Thus the entire top management process—preparation, testing, succession—will become even more problematic than it already is. This may be the most difficult problem ahead in the shift to the information-based organization.

15

MANAGEMENT AS SOCIAL
FUNCTION AND LIBERAL ART

When Karl Marx was beginning work on *Das Kapital* in the 1850s, the phenomenon of management was unknown. So were the enterprises that managers run. The largest manufacturing company around was a Manchester cotton mill employing fewer than three hundred people and owned by Marx's friend and collaborator Friedrich Engels. And in Engels's mill—one of the most profitable businesses of its day—there were no "managers," only "charge hands" who, themselves workers, enforced discipline over a handful of fellow "proletarians."

Rarely in human history has any institution emerged as quickly as management or had as great an impact so fast. In less than one hundred fifty years, management has transformed the social and economic fabric of the world's developed countries. It has created a global economy and set new rules for countries that would participate in that economy as equals. And it has itself been transformed. Few executives are aware of the tremendous impact management has had. Indeed, a good many are like M. Jourdain, the character in

Molière's *Bourgeois Gentilhomme,* who did not know that he spoke prose. They barely realize that they practice—or mispractice—management. As a result, they are ill-prepared for the tremendous challenges that now confront them. The truly important problems managers face do not come from technology or politics; they do not originate outside of management and enterprise. They are problems caused by the very success of management itself.

To be sure, the fundamental task of management remains the same: to make people capable of joint performance through common goals, common values, the right structure, and the training and development they need to perform and to respond to change. But the very meaning of this task has changed, if only because the performance of management has converted the workforce from one composed largely of unskilled laborers to one of highly educated knowledge workers.

The Origins and Development of Management

Eighty years ago, on the threshold of World War I, a few thinkers were just becoming aware of management's existence. But few people even in the most advanced countries had anything to do with it. Now the largest single group in the labor force, more than one third of the total, are people whom the U. S. Bureau of the Census calls "managerial and professional." Management has been the main agent of this transformation. Management explains why, for the first time in human history, we can employ large numbers of knowledgeable, skilled people in productive work. No earlier society could do this. Indeed, no earlier society could support more than a handful of such people. Until quite recently, no one knew how to put people with different skills and knowledge together to achieve common goals. Eighteenth-century China was the envy of contemporary Western intellectuals because it supplied more jobs for educated people than all of Europe did—some twenty thousand per year. Today, the United

States, with about the same population China then had, graduates nearly a million college students a year, few of whom have the slightest difficulty finding well-paid employment. Management enables us to employ them.

Knowledge, especially advanced knowledge, is always specialized. By itself it produces nothing. Yet a modern business, and not only the largest ones, may employ up to ten thousand highly knowledgeable people who represent up to sixty different knowledge areas. Engineers of all sorts, designers, marketing experts, economists, statisticians, psychologists, planners, accountants, human-resources people—all working together in a joint venture. None would be effective without the managed enterprise.

There is no point in asking which came first, the educational explosion of the last one hundred years or the management that put this knowledge to productive use. Modern management and modern enterprise could not exist without the knowledge base that developed societies have built. But equally, it is management, and management alone, that makes effective all this knowledge and these knowledgeable people. The emergence of management has converted knowledge from social ornament and luxury into the true capital of any economy.

Not many business leaders could have predicted this development back in 1870, when large enterprises were first beginning to take shape. The reason was not so much lack of foresight as lack of precedent. At that time, the only large permanent organization around was the army. Not surprisingly, therefore, its command-and-control structure became the model for the men who were putting together transcontinental railroads, steel mills, modern banks, and department stores. The command model, with a very few at the top giving orders and a great many at the bottom obeying them, remained the norm for nearly one hundred years. But it was never as static as its longevity might suggest. On the contrary, it began to change almost at once, as specialized knowledge of all sorts poured into enterprise. The first university-trained engineer in manufacturing industry was hired by Siemens in Germany in 1867—his name was Friedrich von Hefner-Alteneck. Within five years he had built a research department. Other specialized departments followed suit. By World War I the standard functions of a manufacturer had been developed: research and engineering, manufacturing, sales, finance and accounting, and a little later, human resources (or personnel).

Even more important for its impact on enterprise—and on the world economy in general—was another management-directed development that took place at this time. That was the application of management to manual work in the form of training. The child of wartime necessity, training has propelled the transformation of the world economy in the last forty years because it allows low-wage countries to do something that traditional economic theory had said could never be done: to become efficient—and yet still low-wage—competitors almost overnight.

Adam Smith reported that it took several hundred years for a country or region to develop a tradition of labor and the expertise in manual and managerial skills needed to produce and market a given product, whether cotton textiles or violins. During World War I, however, large numbers of unskilled, pre-industrial people had to be made productive workers in practically no time. To meet this need, businesses in the United States and the United Kingdom began to apply the theory of scientific management developed by Frederick W. Taylor between 1885 and 1910 to the systematic training of blue-collar workers on a large scale. They analyzed tasks and broke them down into individual, unskilled operations that could then be learned quite quickly. Further developed in World War II, training was then picked up by the Japanese and, twenty years later, by the South Koreans, who made it the basis for their countries' phenomenal development.

During the 1920s and 1930s, management was applied to many more areas and aspects of the manufacturing business. Decentralization, for instance, arose to combine the advantages of bigness and the advantages of smallness within one enterprise. Accounting went from "bookkeeping" to analysis and control. Planning grew out of the "Gantt charts" designed in 1917 and 1918 to plan war production; and so did the use of analytical logic and statistics, which employ quantification to convert experience and intuition into definitions, information, and diagnosis. Marketing evolved as a result of applying management concepts to distribution and selling. Moreover, as early as the mid-1920s and early 1930s, some American management pioneers such as Thomas Watson, Sr., at the fledgling IBM, Robert E. Wood at Sears, Roebuck, and George Elton Mayo at the Harvard Business School, began to question the way manufacturing was organized. They concluded that the assembly line was a short-term compromise. Despite its tremendous productivity, it was poor economics because of its inflexibility, poor use of human resources, even poor engineering. They began the thinking and experimenting that eventually led to "automation" as the way to organize the manufacturing process, and to teamwork, quality circles, and the information-based organization as the way to manage human resources. Every one of these managerial innovations represented the application of knowledge to work, the substitution of system and information for guesswork, brawn, and toil. Every one, to use Frederick Taylor's term, replaced "working harder" with "working smarter."

The powerful effect of these changes became apparent during World War II. To the very end, the Germans were by far the better strategists. Having much shorter interior lines, they needed fewer support troops and could match their opponents in combat strength. Yet the Allies won—their victory achieved by management. The United States, with one fifth the population of all the other belligerents together, had almost as many men in uniform. Yet it produced more war materiel than all the others taken together. It managed to transport the stuff to fighting fronts as far apart as China, Russia, India, Africa, and Western Europe. No wonder, then, that by the war's end almost all the world had become management-conscious. Or that management emerged as a recognizably distinct kind of work, one that could be studied and developed into a discipline—as happened in each country that has enjoyed economic leadership during the postwar period.

After World War II we began to see that management is not *business* management. It pertains to every human effort that brings together in one organization people of diverse knowledge and skills. It needs to be applied to all third-sector institutions, such as hospitals, universities, churches, arts organizations, and social service agencies, which since World War II have grown faster in the United States than either business or government. For even though the need to manage volunteers or raise funds may differentiate non-profit managers from their for-profit peers, many more of their responsibilities are the same—among them defining the right strategy and goals, developing people, measuring performance, and marketing the organization's services. *Management worldwide has become the new social function.*

Management and Entrepreneurship

One important advance in the discipline and practice of management is that both now embrace entrepreneurship and innovation. A sham fight these days pits "management" against "entrepreneurship" as adversaries, if not as mutually exclusive. That's like saying that the fingering hand and the bow hand of the violinist are "adversaries" or "mutually exclusive." Both are always needed and at the same time. And both have to be coordinated and work together. Any *existing* organization, whether a business, a church, a labor union, or a hospital, goes down fast if it does not innovate. Conversely, any *new* organization, whether a business, a church, a labor union, or a hospital, collapses if it does not manage. Not to innovate is the single largest reason for the decline of existing organizations. Not to know how to manage is the single largest reason for the failure of new ventures.

Yet few management books paid attention to entrepreneurship and innovation. One reason was that during the period after World War II when most of these books were written, managing the existing rather than innovating the new and different was the dominant task. During this period most institutions developed along lines laid down clearly thirty or fifty years earlier. This has now changed dramatically. We have again entered an era of innovation, and it is by no means confined to "high tech" or to technology generally. In fact, social innovation—as this book tries to make clear—may be of greater importance and have much greater impact than any scientific or technical invention. Furthermore, we now have a "discipline" of entrepreneurship and innovation (see my *Innovation and Entrepreneurship,* 1986). It is clearly a part of management and rests, indeed, on well-known and tested management principles. It applies to both existing organizations and new ventures, and to both business and non-business institutions, including government.

The Legitimacy of Management

Management books tend to focus on the function of management inside its organizations. Few yet accept its social function. But it is precisely because management has become so pervasive as a social function that it faces its most serious challenge. To whom is management accountable? And for what? On what does management base its power? What gives it legitimacy?

These are not business questions or economic questions.

227

They are *political* questions. Yet they underlie the most serious assault on management in its history—a far more serious assault than any mounted by Marxists or labor unions: the hostile takeover. An American phenomenon at first, it has spread throughout the non-Communist developed world. What made it possible was the emergence of the employee pension funds as the controlling shareholders of publicly owned companies. The pension funds, while legally "owners," are economically "investors"—and, indeed, often "speculators." They have no interest in the enterprise and its welfare. In fact, in the United States at least they are "trustees," and are not supposed to consider anything but immediate pecuniary gain. What underlies the takeover bid is the postulate that the enterprise's sole function is to provide the largest possible *immediate* gain to the shareholder. In the absence of any other justification for management and enterprise, the "raider" with his hostile takeover bid prevails—and only too often immediately dismantles or loots the going concern, sacrificing long-range, wealth-producing capacity to short-term gains.

Management—and not only in the business enterprise—has to be accountable for performance. But how is performance to be defined? How is it to be measured? How is it to be enforced? And to *whom* should management be accountable? That these questions can be asked is in itself a measure of the success and importance of management. That they need to be asked is, however, also an indictment of managers. They have not yet faced up to the fact that they represent power—and power has to be accountable, has to be legitimate. They have not yet faced up to the fact that they matter.

What Is Management?

But what is management? Is it a bag of techniques and tricks? A bundle of analytical tools like those taught in business schools? These are important, to be sure, just as thermometer and anatomy are important to the physician. But the evolution and history of management—its successes as well as its problems—teach that management is, above all else, a very few, essential principles. To be specific:

• Management is about human beings. Its task is to make people capable of joint performance, to make their strengths effective and their weaknesses irrelevant. This is what organization is all about, and it is the reason that management is the critical, determining factor. These days, practically all of us are employed by managed institutions, large and small, business and non-business. We depend on management for our livelihoods. And our ability to contribute to society also depends as much on the management of the organizations in which we work as it does on our own skills, dedication, and effort.

• Because management deals with the integration of people in a common venture, it is deeply embedded in culture. What managers do in West Germany, in the United Kingdom, in the United States, in Japan, or in Brazil is exactly the same. How they do it may be quite different. Thus one of the basic challenges managers in a developing country face is to find and identify those parts of their own tradition, history, and culture that can be used as management building blocks. The difference between Japan's economic success and India's relative backwardness is largely explained by the fact that Japanese managers were able to plant imported management concepts in their own cultural soil and make them grow.

• Every enterprise requires commitment to common goals and shared values. Without such commitment there is no enterprise, there is only a mob. The enterprise must have simple, clear, and unifying objectives. The mission of the organization has to be clear enough and big enough to provide common vision. The goals that embody it have to be clear, public, and constantly reaffirmed. Management's first job is to think through, set, and exemplify those objectives, values, and goals.

• Management must also enable the enterprise and each of its members to grow and develop as needs and opportunities change. Every enterprise is a learning and teaching institution. Training and development must be built into it on all levels—training and development that never stop.

• Every enterprise is composed of people with different skills and knowledge doing many different kinds of work. It must be built on communication and on individual responsibility. All members need to think through what they aim to accomplish—and make sure that their associates know and understand that aim. All have to think through what they owe to others—and make sure that others understand. All have to think through what they in turn need from others—and make sure that others know what is expected of them.

• Neither the quantity of output nor the "bottom line" is by itself an adequate measure of the performance of management and enterprise. Market standing, innovation, productivity, development of people, quality, financial results—all are crucial to an organization's performance and to its survival. Non-profit institutions too need measurements in a number of areas specific to their mission. Just as a human being needs a diversity of measures to assess his or her health and performance, an organization needs a diversity of measures to assess its health and performance. Performance has to be built into the enterprise and its management; it has to be measured—or at least judged—and it has to be continuously improved.

• Finally, the single most important thing to remember about any enterprise is that results exist only on the outside. The result of a business is a satisfied customer. The result of a hospital is a healed patient. The result of a school is a student who has learned something and puts it to work ten years later. Inside an enterprise, there are only costs.

230

Managers who understand these principles and function in their light will be achieving, accomplished managers.

Management as a Liberal Art

Thirty years ago, the English scientist and novelist C. P. Snow talked of the "two cultures" of contemporary society. Management, however, fits neither Snow's "humanist" nor his "scientist." It deals with action and application; and its test are results. This makes it a technology. But management also deals with people, their values, their growth and development—and this makes it a humanity. So does its concern with, and impact on, social structure and the community. Indeed, as everyone has learned who, like this author, has been working with managers of all kinds of institutions for long years, management is deeply involved in spiritual concerns—the nature of man, good and evil.

Management is thus what tradition used to call a liberal art—"liberal" because it deals with the fundamentals of knowledge, self-knowledge, wisdom, and leadership; "art" because it is practice and application. Managers draw on all the knowledges and insights of the humanities and the social sciences—on psychology and philosophy, on economics and history, on the physical sciences and ethics. But they have to focus this knowledge on effectiveness and results—on healing a sick patient, teaching a student, building a bridge, designing and selling a "user-friendly" software program.

For these reasons, management will increasingly be the discipline and the practice through which the "humanities" will again acquire recognition, impact, and relevance.

16

THE SHIFTING KNOWLEDGE BASE

Within the next decades education will change more than it has changed since the modern school was created by the printed book over three hundred years ago. An economy in which knowledge is becoming the true capital and the premier wealth-producing resource makes new and stringent demands on the schools for educational performance and educational responsibility. A society dominated by knowledge workers makes even newer—and even more stringent—demands for social performance and social responsibility. Once again we will have to think through what an educated person is. At the same time, how we learn and how we teach are changing drastically and fast—the result, in part, of new theoretical understanding of the learning process, in part of new technology. Finally, many of the traditional disciplines of the schools are becoming sterile, if not obsolescent. We thus also face changes in *what* we learn and teach and, indeed, in what we mean by knowledge.

Educational Responsibilities

Since school learning and school diplomas increasingly control access to jobs, livelihoods, and careers in the knowledge society, all members of society need to be literate. And not only in "reading, writing, and arithmetic." Literacy now includes elementary computer skills. It requires a considerable understanding of technology, its dimensions, its characteristics, its rhythms—something almost totally absent today in any country. It requires considerable knowledge of a complex world in which boundaries of town, nation, and country no longer define one's horizons. For this reason, knowledge of one's roots and community is however also becoming more important. The new media provide quite a bit of this new literacy. For today's small child, the television set and the video cassette recorder surely provide as much information as does the school—in fact probably more. But only through the school—through organized, systematic, purposeful learning—can this information be converted into knowledge and become the individual's possession and tool.

The knowledge society also requires that all its members learn how to learn. It is of the very nature of knowledge that it changes fast. Manual skills change very slowly. Socrates the stonemason—the trade in which he made his living—would be at home in a modern mason's yard. But Socrates the philosopher would be totally baffled by both the concerns and the tools of such key disciplines of modern philosophy as symbolic logic or linguistics. Engineers ten years out of school are already "obsolescent" if they have not refreshed their knowledge again and again. And so are the physician, lawyer, teacher, geologist, manager, and computer programmer. Furthermore, there is an infinity of knowledge careers to choose from. There is no way in which even the best school system with the longest years of schooling can possibly prepare students for all these choices. All it can do is to prepare

233

them to learn. The post-business, knowledge society is a society of continuing learning and second careers.

The American School and Its Priorities

Plenty of school systems around the world provide universal literacy (although so far only in its traditional form): all of Northern and Western Europe, Japan, Korea. Not so long ago—until 1960—so did the American school. It no longer does. Whatever the reason—and a major one is surely that it subordinated its teaching mission to other socially necessary objectives—the American school has become untrue to its educational responsibility. The failure of the American school to deliver universal literacy is America's real "Rust Belt." It is a far greater weakness than high cost and poor quality in consumer products. In the knowledge society, the knowledge base is the foundation of the economy.

Thirty years ago, in the years after World War II, the American school led. Some of the "best" schools in other countries were probably better than the "best" schools of the America of 1960. But no other country then had as high a general level. Just as American industrial leadership made American manufacturers complacent, however, American educational leadership thirty years ago made American educators complacent. To restore the capacity of the American school to provide universal literacy on a high level—well beyond that of the elementary school—will therefore have to be a first priority. School and education will be central to American public life and American politics for years to come.

We actually know pretty much what is required. The job is not even so very difficult. It is, however, highly political. It requires high standards and a good deal of discipline in the schools. This will be demanded (it is already being demanded) by parents who are themselves reasonably well educated and have children ready to learn. But standards and discipline are being resisted by some parents of the very children who need them most—especially by some of the parents of poor minority children. They see in such demands "racism" and "discrimination." This is already happening not only in the United States but at the universities in West Germany where the New Left gained power during the sixties (in Bremen, for example). Just as graduates of America's "problem schools" are shunned by prospective employers, so are the graduates of Germany's "problem universities."

America is the only major developed country in which there is no competition within the school system. The French have two parallel systems above the elementary grades, a public and a Catholic one, both paid for by the state. So do the Italians. Germany has the *Gymnasium,* the college-preparatory school for a fairly small elite. In Japan, schools are graded by the performance of their students on the university entrance exams. The teachers of high-ranking schools are recognized, promoted, and paid accordingly. The American public school, by contrast, has a near-monopoly—no performance standards and little competition either within the system or from the outside. This is already changing. In Minnesota—traditionally a pioneer in social innovation—parents can now place their child in any school in the state, with the state reimbursing the school district for any child it admits from outside. This is a first step toward a voucher system under which the state pays a child's tuition to any accredited school the child and its parents choose. The public school lobby strongly resists the idea. But how long can it prevail?

By common consent the public schools of Chicago are among the worst in the country. Next door to them are the parochial schools of the Chicago Catholic Diocese in which black children from Chicago's worst slums actually learn successfully. These achieving schools are in constant financial danger. Yet for black parents in Chicago's inner city, even the very modest fees they charge impose a real sacrifice. Chicago has only two choices: either it issues vouchers which enable

Chicago's blacks to send their children to the schools where they learn something or—and it is already happening—resistance of Chicago's blacks (and that means of the largest single voting bloc in the city) to school taxes slowly liquidates the city's public schools. Chicago's whites, rich or poor, have long deserted the city's public schools. They have either moved out into suburbs with decent schools or have put their children into private schools where there are standards, discipline, and learning.

In Rochester, New York, the American Federation of Teachers negotiated a new contract in 1984 with the city. It provides for more money but only for teachers who meet high and rising performance standards. It also provides for dismissal of those who do *not* meet performance standards. And wherever we have built discipline, performance standards, and competition into a school it has performed—not miracles, to be sure, but an acceptable quality job of delivering universal literacy.

Learning How to Learn

Delivering literacy—even on the high level appropriate to a knowledge society—will be an easier task than giving students the capacity and the knowledge to keep on learning, and the desire to do it. No school system has yet tackled that job. There is an old Latin tag: *Non schola sed vita discimus* (We don't learn for school but for life). But neither teacher nor student has ever taken it seriously. Indeed, except for professional schools—medicine, law, engineering, business—no school to the best of my knowledge has even tried to find out what its students have learned. We compile voluminous records of examination results. But I know of no school that tests the graduates ten years later on what they still know of the subjects—whether mathematics, a foreign language, or history—in which they got such wonderful marks. We do know, however, how people learn how to learn. In fact, we have known it for two thousand years. The first and wisest writer on raising small children, the great Greek biographer and historian Plutarch, spelled it out in a charming little book, *Paidea (Raising Children),* in the first century of the Christian era. All.it requires is to make learners achieve. All it requires is to focus on the strengths and talents of learners so that they excel in whatever it is they do well. Any teacher of young artists—musicians, actors, painters—knows this. So does any teacher of young athletes. But schools do not do it. They focus instead on a learner's weaknesses.

When teachers call in the parents of a ten-year-old, they usually say: "Your Jimmy has to work on the multiplication tables. He is way behind." They rarely say: "Your Mary should do a good deal more writing to do even better what she already does well." Teachers—and this goes right through to the university—tend to focus on the weaknesses of students, and for good reasons: no one can predict what a ten-year-old will be doing ten or fifteen years later. One cannot even at that stage eliminate many options. The school has to endow students with the basic skills they will need whichever way they choose to go. They have to be able to function. But one cannot build performance on weaknesses, even on corrected ones; one can build performance only on strengths. And these the schools traditionally ignore, in fact, consider more or less irrelevant. Strengths do not create problems— and schools are problem-focused.

In the knowledge society, teachers will have to learn to say: "I am going to make your Jimmy, or your Mary, do a great deal more writing. The child has talent that needs to be developed and perfected." As will be discussed a little further on, the new technology of teaching will make this possible; indeed, in large measure it will almost demand a focus on strength.

But the educational system we need will also have to stress the responsibility of knowledge. "Knowledge is power" is an old saw—for the first time there is some truth to it. The knowledge workers in their entirety will be the "rulers." They will also have to be the "leaders." That requires ethos, values, and morality. "Moral education" today has fallen into disrepute. Far too often it was abused in order to stifle thinking, discussion, and dissent, and to inculcate blind obedience to authority. Far too often in fact it became "immoral education." But every one of the education builders discussed below—from Confucius to Arnold of Rugby—knew that there is no education without moral values. To slough off moral values as modern education proposes to do only means that education conveys the wrong values. It conveys indifference, irresponsibility, cynicism. Precisely what the moral values of education in the knowledge society have to be will be hotly debated. But education in moral values, and the commitment to moral values, will be central. Knowledge people have to learn to take responsibility.

Education as Social Purpose

Most schools these days in developed and developing countries alike teach the same subjects. Methods of instruction do not, as a rule, change over centuries. But though the schools themselves may look very much the same, the social purpose of education—the society it attempts to shape and the rulers and leaders it aims to form—varies widely.

The clearest concept of education's social purpose is also the oldest one: the Chinese ideal of the Confucian scholar and gentleman as the ruler. Formulated well before the Christian era and codified no later than the T'ang Dynasty of the seventh century A.D., it survived unchanged into recent times. Advanced education in Communist China today is still very much Confucian in structure and basic values, even though no longer Confucian in content.

In the West a similar formulation was not attempted until the late sixteenth and early seventeenth centuries. The Jesuits then first saw that the printed book made it possible for them to obtain political and social control of society through a monopoly on advanced education. They designed the first modern school to make themselves masters of the high-born and of the learned. A little later a Czech, John Amos Comenius—the first person to advocate universal literacy—invented the textbook and the primer. These, he hoped, would enable his compatriots to remain Protestants despite political domination by the fiercely Catholic Habsburgs. Literacy, Comenius argued, enables people to read the Bible in their homes. A substantial minority in Czechoslovakia has indeed remained Protestant to this day.

In the eighteenth century the entire West accepted that education and schools are major social forces. Colonial America, strongly influenced by Comenius, designed its school from the beginning to be the maker of citizens. Thomas Jefferson's educational outline for Virginia—the most comprehensive strategy for education since the Confucians in China—was universal, classless, and yet designed to produce a democratic elite. When, in the nineteenth century, immigration swelled to a flood, the American school became the agent of Americanization for the newcomers and the teacher of the American creed. It was its success in this role more than any other factor that made us choose it as the agent of racial integration a century later.

At about the same time the American colonists developed their system of universal education, such a system was also designed in Europe—by the eighteenth-century Emperor Joseph II of Austria. Joseph II focused on advanced schooling—the "gymnasium"—as central to his social policy. It taught the same subjects as the schools of the Jesuits or the schools of the American colonists. But its aims were different. Joseph set out to wrest control of education away from the Catholic Church; to make sure that educated people were secular in their orientation and anti-clerical; and to provide social mobility to able young commoners. The Austrian gymnasium is one of the success stories of education as a social agent. It held Austria together for one hundred fifty years despite increasing nationalist conflicts and tensions. Its graduates, even though taught in all the many languages of the empire, held the same values and shared the same ethos. They constituted an educated ruling class that worked together across the barriers of language and national origin until the empire collapsed in 1918.

At about the same time—in the mid-eighteenth century—the *Bunjin* (i.e., "literati" or humanists) of far-away Japan used education to create a new vision and a new social class. They rejected the official hierarchy based on birth, with its three hereditary classes of swordsman (samurai), peasant, and townsman, replacing it with a meritocracy in which nothing counted except performance as a scholar, calligrapher, and artist. They thus laid the foundations for modern Japan. A hundred years later, in 1867, when the feudal regime of the Tokugawa Shōgun fell and the Meiji Restoration began, every one of the new leaders was a graduate of an academy founded seventy years earlier by such eminent *Bunjin* as the calligrapher-painters Nukina Kaioku and Rai Sanyo.

Napoleon I deliberately fashioned educational institutions to create a new and different France. He was not even emperor when he founded the *grandes écoles* as schools for a new elite. The *Ecole Normale* for teachers and the *Polytechnique* for engineers were to make sure that France could not return to the society and government of pre-Revolutionary days. They were to give France a ruling class of high talent—non-aristocratic, anti-clerical, and nationalist. To this day the *grandes écoles* form the French ruling elites, and with them the basic values and vision of French government and French society.

A few years later, but still during the Napoleonic wars, Wilhelm von Humboldt—the Prussian statesman and great scholar who pioneered modern linguistics—founded the first modern university in 1809. Designed as an answer to Napoleon, Humboldt's University of Berlin, like Napoleon's *grandes écoles,* was to educate an elite composed of commoners. But the purpose was not to prevent a return to the Ancien Régime but to enable such a regime to rule over the post-Revolutionary society. The task of Humboldt's university was to give society a sphere of intellectual freedom. There would be another sphere of freedom, the market economy. Together the two would support an absolute monarchy and enable it to survive. This was the *Rechtsstaat,* the political system in which the "King under the Law" rather than "the people" was to rule. In one form or another it survived in Germany until 1918. Indeed, it was not truly buried until the coming of the Nazis in 1933.

The last shaper of modern advanced education was Dr. Thomas Arnold, the famous "Arnold of Rugby." Every earlier system of advanced education—Chinese, American, Austrian, Japanese, French, German—saw the school as the agent of social mobility through which the able and achieving could rise out of the "lower classes" into gentility and social position. Arnold's public school, however, was designed to perpetuate the class system. It was a school to educate "gentlemen"; and "gentlemen" are born rather than made by schooling. By making the public school a boarding school for the well-born, Arnold made England's school system a barrier to social mobility. It has often been pointed out that by any measurement there was more social mobility in England in the nineteenth century than in any other Western country except the United States. Yet England suffers to this day from acute class-consciousness and class feeling. For alone among the systems of advanced education, the English school system did not admit, let alone recruit, the able and achieving youngsters of the lower classes for advancement into the leadership groups or at least into social respectability. (In Scotland, by contrast, school and university were developed in the eighteenth century to be powerfully effective agents of social mobility.)

The New Requirements

There will be—and there should be—serious discussion of the social purpose and responsibility of education in the new reality of the knowledge society. This is much too important a decision to be made by acclamation—or by not making it. A few key requirements are already clear:

• Education in and for the knowledge society will have a social purpose. It will not be value-free; no educational system has ever been.

• The educational system needed must be an open system. It must not make into an impenetrable barrier the line between the highly schooled and the "other half." Able and achieving people need to have access to education and, through it, to upward mobility, whatever their origin, wealth, or previous schooling. There are some beginnings. In Japan, for instance, teachers are expected to look after the promising young people in their class and make sure that they do well enough scholastically to advance from elementary school to middle school, from middle school to high school, and eventually from high school to university. Teachers in Japan are as much counselors to the student and to the student's family as they are teachers in the classroom. West Germany has used its traditional apprentice training to create parallel ladders of scholastic advancement. One leads from the academically oriented secondary school—the traditional *Gymnasium*—to the university. The other starts with the apprentice program in which the young man or woman works three days a week and goes to school three days a week, thus obtaining both a practical and a theoretical foundation. This then enables them to go on to a *Fachhochschule* and obtain an academic diploma which opens opportunities for advancement, especially in business.

But the most promising of these approaches so far is the American one. In every other educational system, the student has to get the appropriate diploma at the appropriate age—for junior high school or middle school, for high school, or for college. In Germany, students can stay at the university for seven or ten years—or forever. But unless they enter at age nineteen or twenty, they will rarely get in. The same is largely true in Japan, in Great Britain, and in France. In the United States, students who dropped out of high school are encouraged to come back and get their high school or college diplomas years later.

• In the traditional system, each school sees itself as terminal. Once students have sat through enough semesters, their education is "finished." There is no such thing as a "finished education" in the knowledge society. It requires that people with advanced schooling come back to school again and again and again. Continuing education, especially of highly schooled people such as physicians, teachers, scientists, managers, engineers, and accountants, is certain to be a major growth industry of the future. So far, however, schools and universities, except in the United States and Great Britain to a degree, still view continuing education with grave misgivings if they do not shun it altogether.

• Education can no longer be confined to the schools. Every employing institution has to become a teacher. Large Japanese employers—government agencies and businesses—already recognize this. The country that is again in the lead, however, is the United States, where employers—business, government agencies, the military—spend as much money and effort on the education and training of their employees, and especially the most highly educated ones, as do all the

243

country's colleges and universities together. European transnational companies too are increasingly taking on the continuing education of their employees and especially of managers.

• Finally, it will be the social responsibility of education to prevent "meritocracy" from degenerating into "plutocracy." To make access to good jobs and careers dependent upon the diploma is tolerable only if the diploma is given for talent and diligence rather than for wealth. Care must be taken lest the diploma becomes a barrier to ability rather than a recognition thereof. It must not become a symbol of "class," as Dr. Arnold's public school became in England. This threat is already reality in the most "meritocratic" country: Japan. The Japanese university charges no or very low tuition; yet increasingly it is the children of the wealthy who get into the prestige universities and thus gain access to the promising careers in both government and industry. Young Japanese do not have much chance to pass the university entrance examinations unless they have a room to themselves at home in which to study. In a country with crowded housing, only fairly well-to-do people can afford so much space.

Children of well-to-do-parents and children of parents who themselves have been highly educated will always have an advantage. But this advantage must not become an insurmountable obstacle to others. One way—in the United States it would be the most effective way—is to make the costs of advanced education repayable out of the graduate's life earnings. No investment in the modern economy pays as well as the advanced degree. There is therefore no reason for taxpayers to subsidize students. But while they are still students they do not have the money. Justice, equity, and economics all demand that they should repay society out of the additional earnings their advanced degree procures for them during their lifetime.

The Educated Person

Education fuels the economy. It shapes society. But it does so through its "product," the educated person.

An educated person is equipped both to lead a life and to make a living. Socrates and Arnold of Rugby put all their emphasis on the "life," and dismissed "making a living" as irrelevant if not vulgar. But very few people in any society have as few wants as Socrates the philosopher, or were endowed with the rich fathers of Arnold's "gentlemen." All other educational philosophies always balanced the two. So will education in the knowledge society. It can afford neither the schooled barbarian who makes a good living but has no life worth living, nor the cultured amateur who lacks commitment and effectiveness. In the knowledge society, education will have to transmit "virtue" while teaching the skills of effectiveness. At present our educational systems do neither—precisely because we have not asked: What is an educated person in the knowledge society?

One hears a great many complaints these days, especially in the United States, about the decline if not disappearance of the "humanities." Any number of books bewail the ignorance of the great traditions on which civilization and culture rest. These complaints are valid. There is danger of producing a society of schooled barbarians. But whose fault is it? The young these days it is said are not attracted to the "classics"; they are said to be "anti-historical." But they do respond with enthusiasm to history, to the great tradition altogether, if offered to them in a form that makes it relevant to their experiences, their society, their needs. Older people, the participants in continuing education, usually cannot get enough of ethics, of history, of great novels, of anything that helps them understand their own experience, the challenges they face in their own life and in their own work. And they also

245

crave the fundamentals of science and technology, the ways and values of government and politics; in short, everything that constitutes a broad liberal education.

But we have to make all this meaningful and to project it on the realities in which people live. There is need to make the "humanities" again what they are supposed to be: lights to help us see and guides to right action. This is not the job of the student; it has to be the job of the teacher. Sixty years ago, in 1927, a French philosopher, Julien Benda, published a slashing attack, *La Trahison des clercs (The Betrayal of the Intellectuals)* on the scholars and writers of his time who subordinated truth to racial and political dogmas, whether of the right or left. Benda's attack was prophetic, anticipating both the betrayal of the truth by the German intellectuals during the Hitler years and the betrayal of the truth by the fellow travelers and Stalinists in the thirties and for twenty or thirty years after World War II. To let the humanities die out of snobbery, disdain, or sloth is equally betrayal. The advent of the knowledge society will force us to focus the wisdom and beauty of the past on the needs and ugliness of the present. This is what scholars and humanists contribute to the making of a life.

The key to doing this may be the needs we face in equipping students to make a living. For almost nothing in our educational systems prepares them for the reality in which they will live, work, and become effective. Our schools have yet to accept the fact that in the knowledge society the majority of people make their living as employees. They work in an organization. They have to be effective in it. This is the exact opposite of what educational systems still assume. Arnold's public school was based on the assumption that its graduates would be leaders in society; it did not expect them to be "employees." The product of the American university or the German university, the professionals, were equipped to earn a living as an independent, or, at most, while working in a small partnership. No educational institution—not even the graduate school of management—tries to equip students with the elementary skills of effectiveness as members of an organization: ability to present ideas orally and in writing (briefly, simply, clearly); ability to work with people; ability to shape and direct one's own work, contribution, career; and generally skills in making organization a tool for one's own aspirations and achievements and for the realization of values. These, by the way, are very much the concerns that Socrates in Plato's Dialogues talked about 2,500 years ago as the keys to a life worth living.

From Teaching to Learning

We now know how people learn. We now know that learning and teaching are not two sides of the same coin—they are different processes. What can be taught has to be taught and will not be learned otherwise. But what can be learned must be learned and cannot be taught. This new insight will increasingly shift the emphasis to learning. For several thousand years the focus has been on teaching; master teachers today teach the same way master teachers taught three thousand years ago. No one has yet found a method to replicate what they are doing. But not until the very end of the nineteenth century was the question ever asked: How do we learn? Once asked, however, new knowledge and new insight accumulated fast.

Since new knowledge always take a long time before it becomes technology and application, we know a great deal more about learning than the schools have so far put to work. But we are at the point now at which the new knowledge of learning is becoming application. We know first that different people learn differently. Indeed, learning is as personal as fingerprints; no two people learn exactly alike. Each has a different speed, a different rhythm, a different attention span. If an alien speed, rhythm, or attention span is imposed on the learner, there is little or no learning; there are only fatigue and resistance. But we also know that different people learn different subjects differently. Most of us learned the multiplication table behaviorally, that is, by drill and repetition. But mathematicians do not "learn" the multiplication table; they perceive it. Similarly, musicians do not learn to read notation; they perceive it. And no born athlete ever had to learn how to catch a ball. Some things do have to be taught— and not only values, insight, meaning. A teacher is needed to identify a child's strengths and to direct a talent toward achievement. Even Mozart would not have become the great genius he was but for a father who was a master teacher.

One learns a subject. One teaches a person.

We are ready now to put this new knowledge into practice. One reason is demographics. In developed countries most people live in metropolitan areas. Thus the learner is no longer confined to the one school with its one learning and teaching pedagogy for everybody, which was all the small village could support. The learner can choose between schools within easy reach, on foot, by bicycle, or by bus, yet each offering a different learning environment. It will predictably become the responsibility of tomorrow's teacher to identify the way learners learn and to direct them to whichever of the available schools best fits their individual learning profiles.

The New Learning Technology

The new technology will force us to make that shift, for it is a learning rather than a teaching technology. As was first pointed out forty years ago by the Canadian Marshall McLuhan, it was not the Renaissance that changed the medieval university. It was the printed book. McLuhan's well-known saying, "The medium is the message," is surely an exaggeration. But the "medium" does imply what message can be sent and received. Equally important, it determines what messages *cannot* be sent and received. And the medium is rapidly changing. Just as the printed book became the new "high tech" of education in the fifteenth century, so computer, television, and video cassettes are becoming the high tech of education in the twentieth century. Thus the new technology is bound to have a profound impact on the schools and how we learn.

The printed book, fiercely resisted by the schoolmasters of the fifteenth and sixteenth centuries, did not triumph until the Jesuits and Comenius created schools based on it in the early seventeenth century. From the beginning the printed book forced the schools however to change drastically how they were teaching. Before then, the only way to learn was either by laboriously copying manuscripts or by listening to lectures and recitations. Suddenly, people could learn by reading. We are in the early stages of a similar technological revolution, and perhaps an even bigger one. The computer is infinitely more "user-friendly" than the printed book, especially for children. It has unlimited patience. No matter how many mistakes the user makes, the computer will be ready for another try. It is at the command of the learner the way no teacher in a classroom can be. Teachers in a busy classroom rarely have time for any one child. The computer by contrast is always there, whether the child is fast, slow, or average; whether it finds this subject difficult and that one easy; whether it wants to learn new things or to go back over something learned earlier. And, unlike the printed book, the computer admits of infinite variation. It is playful.

But also there is television, and with it a whole world of visual pedagogy. There are more hours of pedagogy in one thirty-second commercial than most teachers can pack into a month of teaching. The subject matter of the TV commercial is quite secondary; what matters is the skill, professionalism, and persuasive power of the presentation. Children therefore come to school today with expectations that are bound to be disappointed and frustrated. They expect a level of teaching competence that goes beyond what most teachers can possi-

bly muster. Schools will increasingly be forced to use computers, television, films, video tapes, and audio tapes. The
teacher increasingly will become a supervisor and a mentor—
very much, perhaps, the way he functioned in the medieval
university some hundreds of years ago. The teacher's job will
be to help, to lead, to set example, to encourage; it may not
primarily be to convey the subject matter itself.

The printed book in the West triggered a surge in the love
of learning such as the world had never seen before and has
never seen since. It made it possible for people in all walks of
life to learn at their own speed, in the privacy of their own
home, or in the congenial company of like-minded readers. It
also made it possible for people who were separated from
each other by distance and geography to learn together. In
the West at least the decisive event that produced "learning"
was not the "rediscovery of antiquity"—it had never been
lost. It was the new technology of the printed book. Will
computers and technology together produce a similar explosion of the love of learning? Anyone who has seen a seven-
or eight-year-old spend an hour running a math program on
a computer or an even younger child watching "Sesame
Street" knows that the powder for such an explosion is ac-
cumulating. Even if the schools do their worst to squelch it,
the joy of learning generated by the new technologies will
have an impact. In the United States and in Japan the schools,
after thirty years of fierce resistance to the new technologies,
are increasingly willing to use them, to embody them in their
teaching methods, and to create the desire to learn which, in
the last analysis, is the essence of being educated.

What Is Knowledge?

When the printed book appeared in the fifteenth century,
what comprised "knowledge" was as ready for a sea change
as the methods for transmitting it. We may be at a similar
turning point. Like the Scholastics when the printed book

appeared, we have had two hundred years in which specialization was the royal road both to the acquisition of new knowledge and to its transmission. In the physical sciences that may still work. Elsewhere specialization is becoming an obstacle to the acquisition of knowledge and an even greater barrier to making it effective. Academia defines knowledge as what gets printed. But surely this is not knowledge; it is raw data. Knowledge is information that changes something or somebody—either by becoming grounds for action, or by making an individual (or an institution) capable of different and more effective action. And this, little of the new "knowledge" accomplishes.

Only fifty years ago the great scholars of the day wrote best sellers. Neither John Maynard Keynes nor Joseph Schumpeter—this century's two great economists—were "popularizers." Both were however avidly read by a great many non-economists. Arnold Toynbee, the English historian, did not attempt to cater to the multitude in the 1930s, nor did the books on the Greeks by two great classicists, Edith Hamilton and Werner Jaeger. Yet their works regularly made the best-seller lists, as did those of the leading American historians of the day. Their successors today have to pay to have their papers published in learned journals which not even their colleagues read. We no longer accept the old axiom that it is the duty of people of knowledge to make themselves understood. But until this has been done, no knowledge will have been produced. The readers are there, are indeed waiting hungrily. Whenever good scholars—the American historian Barbara Tuchman, the French historian Fernand Braudel, the English astrophysicist Stephen W. Hawking—deign to present their work in decent prose, the book is an instant hit.

Who or what is to blame for the obscurantism of the learned is beside the point. What matters is that the learning of the academic specialist is rapidly ceasing to be "knowledge." It is at best "erudition" and at its more common worst mere "data." The disciplines and the methods that produced knowledge for two hundred years are no longer fully productive, at least outside of the natural sciences. The rapid growth of cross-disciplinary and interdisciplinary work would indeed argue that new knowledge is no longer obtained from within the disciplines around which teaching, learning, and research have been organized in the nineteenth and twentieth centuries.

In 1943, the German-Swiss novelist Hermann Hesse published his last book, *Das Glasperlenspiel (Magister Ludi)*. He invented a secluded order of intellectuals who spend their time playing Chinese music and puzzling out obscure riddles such as the glass bead game of the title, whilst avoiding any contact with the vulgar world outside. What Hesse had in mind was the withdrawal of German thinkers and writers into an inner world of refinement during the Nazi period. But in the end, Hesse's hero rejects the "internal exile" of the intellectual games and returns to the dirty, noisy, polluted, and corrupt world of real people and therefore of real knowledge. Our academics do not have the excuse the German-speaking intellectuals had in Hitler's day, but they have largely retired into Hesse's glass bead game. Will they now be forced to make knowledge effective again, to make it once again true knowledge?

That major changes are ahead for schools and education is certain—the knowledge society will demand them and the new learning theories and learning technologies will trigger them. How fast they will come we do not, of course, know. But we can predict with high probability *where* they will occur first and hit the hardest: the United States. In part because the United States has the most open, most flexible educational system and the least centralized and regimented one. In part, however, also because it is least satisfied with what it has today—and with good reason.

CONCLUSION

FROM ANALYSIS TO PERCEPTION,
THE NEW WORLD VIEW

Around 1680 a French physicist, Denis Papin, then working in Germany—as a Protestant he had been forced to leave his native country—invented the steam engine. Whether he actually built one we do not know; but he designed one, and he actually put together the first safety valve. A generation later, in 1712, Thomas Newcomen then put the first working steam engine into an English coal mine. This made it possible for coal to be mined—until then groundwater had always flooded English mines. With Newcomen's engine, the age of steam was on. Thereafter, for two hundred fifty years, the model of technology was mechanical. Fossil fuels rapidly became the main source of energy. And the ultimate source of motive power was what happens inside a star, that is, the sun. In 1945, atomic fission and, a few years later, fusion replicated what occurs in the sun. There is no going beyond this. In 1945 the era in which the mechanical universe was the model came to an end. Just a year later, in 1946, the first computer, the ENIAC, came on stream. And with it began an age in which information will be the organizing principle for work. Information, however, is the basic principle of biological rather than of mechanical processes.

Very few events have as much impact on civilization as a change in the basic principle for organizing work. Up until A.D. 800 or 900, China was far ahead of any Western country in technology, in science, and in culture and civilization generally. Then the Benedictine monks in Northern Europe found new sources of energy. Until that point the main source of energy, if not the only one, had been a two-legged animal called man. It was the peasant's wife who pulled the plow. The horse collar for the first time made it possible to replace the farmer's wife with animal power. And the Benedictines also converted what in antiquity were toys, waterwheel and windmill, into the first machines. Within two hundred years, technological leadership shifted from China to the Occident. Seven hundred years later Papin's steam engine created a new technology and with it a new world view—the mechanical universe.

In 1946, with the advent of the computer, information became the organizing principle of production. With this, a new basic civilization came into being.

The Social Impacts of Information

A great deal these days (almost too much) is being said and written about the impact of the information technologies on the material civilization, on goods, services, and businesses. The social impacts are, however, as important; indeed, they may be more important. One of the impacts is widely noticed: any such change triggers an explosion of entrepreneurship. In fact the entrepreneurial surge which began in the United States in the late 1970s, and which within ten years had spread to all non-Communist developed countries, is the fourth such surge since Denis Papin's time three hundred years ago. The first one ran from the middle of the seventeenth century through the early years of the eighteenth century; it was triggered by the "Commercial Revolution," the tremendous expansion of trade following the development of the first ocean-going freighter that could actually carry heavy payloads over large distances. The second entrepreneurial surge—beginning in the middle of the eighteenth century and running to the middle of the nineteenth—was what we commonly call the "Industrial Revolution." Then, around 1870, the third entrepreneurial surge was triggered by the new industries—the first ones that did not just apply different motive power but actually turned out products that had never been made before or only in minute quantities: electricity, telephone, electronics, steel, chemicals and pharmaceuticals, automobiles and aeroplanes.

We are now in a fourth surge, triggered by information and biology. Like the earlier entrepreneurial surges, the present one is not confined to "high tech"; it embraces equally "middle tech," "low tech," and "no tech." Like the earlier ones, it is not confined to new or small enterprises, but is carried by existing and big ones as well—and often with the greatest impact and effectiveness. And, like the earlier surges, it is not confined to "inventions," that is, to technology. Social innovations are equally "entrepreneurial" and equally important. Some of the social innovations of the Industrial Revolution—the modern army, the civil service, the Post Office, the commercial bank—have surely had as much impact as railroad or steamship. Similarly, the present age of entrepreneurship will be as important for its social innovations—and especially for innovations in politics, government, education, and economics—as for any new technology or material product.

Another important social impact of information is also visible and widely discussed: the impact on the national state and, particularly, on that twentieth-century hypertrophy of the national state, the totalitarian regime. Itself a creature of the modern media, newspapers, movies, and radio, it can exist

257

only if it has total control of information. But with everyone being able to receive information directly from a satellite in the home—and on "dishes" already so small that no secret police can hope to find them—control of information by government is no longer possible. Indeed, information is now transnational; like money, information has no "fatherland."

Since information knows no national boundaries, it will also form new "transnational" communities of people who, maybe without ever seeing each other in the flesh, are in communion because they are in communication. The world economy, especially the "symbol economy" of money and credit, is already one of the non-national, transnational communities.

Other social impacts are just as important but rarely seen or discussed. One of them is the likely transformation of the twentieth-century city. Today's city was created by the great breakthrough of the nineteenth century: the ability to move people to work by means of train and streetcar, bicycle and automobile. It will be transformed by the great twentieth-century breakthrough: the ability to move work to people by moving ideas and information. In fact, the city—central Tokyo, central New York, central Los Angeles, central London, central Paris, central Bombay—has already outlived its usefulness. We no longer can move people into and out of it, as witness the two-hour trips in packed railroad carriages to reach the Tokyo or New York office building, the chaos in London's Piccadilly Circus, or the two-hour traffic jams on the Los Angeles freeways every morning and evening. We are already beginning to move the information to where the people are—outside the cities—in such work as the handling of credit cards, of engineering designs, of insurance policies and insurance claims, or of medical records. Increasingly people will work in their homes or, as many more are likely to do, in small "office satellites" outside the crowded central city. The facsimile machine, the telephone, the two-way video screen, the telex, the teleconference are taking over from railroad, automobile, and from airplane as well. The real-estate boom in all the big cities in the seventies and eighties, and the attendant skyscraper explosion, are not signs of health. They signal the beginning of the end of the central city. The decline may be slow; but we no longer need that great achievement, the central city, at least not in its present form.

The city might become an information center rather than a center for work—the place from which information (news, data, music) radiates. It might resemble the medieval cathedral where the peasants from the surrounding countryside congregated once or twice a year at the great feast days; in between it stood empty except for its learned clerics and its cathedral school. And will tomorrow's university be a "knowledge center" that transmits information, rather than a place that students actually attend?

Where work is done determines in large measure also how it is done. It strongly affects what work is being done. That there will be great changes we can be certain—but how and when so far we cannot even guess.

Form and Function

The question of the right size for a given task or a given organization will become a central challenge. Greater performance in a mechanical system is obtained by scaling up. Greater power means greater output: bigger is better. But this does not hold for biological systems. There size follows function. It would surely be counterproductive for the cockroach to be big, and equally counterproductive for the elephant to be small. As biologists are fond of saying, "The rat knows everything it needs to be successful as a rat." Whether the rat is more intelligent than the human being is a stupid question; in what it takes to be successful as a rat, the rat is way ahead of any other animal, including the human being. (The best book on this is *On Growth and Form,* written in 1917 by the

Scottish biologist Sir D'Arcy Wentworth Thompson—a "must" for anyone concerned with organization design and organization structure.) In an information-based society, bigness becomes a "function" and a dependent, rather than an independent, variable. In fact the characteristics of information imply that the smallest effective size will be best. "Bigger" will be "better" only if the task cannot be done otherwise.

For communication to be effective there has to be both information and meaning. And meaning requires communion. If somebody whose language I do not speak calls me on the telephone, it doesn't help me at all that the connection is crystal clear. There is no "meaning" unless I understand the language—the message the meteorologist understands perfectly is gibberish to a chemist. Communion, however, does not work well if the group is very large. It requires constant reaffirmation. It requires the ability to interpret. It requires a community. "I know what this message means because I know how our people think in Tokyo, or in London, or in Beijing." *I know* is the catalyst that converts "information" into "communications."

For fifty years, from the early days of the Great Depression to the 1970s, the trend ran toward centralization and bigness. Prior to 1929, doctors did not put their paying patients into hospitals except for surgery. Very few babies before the 1920s were born in hospitals; the majority were born at home. The dynamics of higher education in the United States as late as the 1930s were in the small and medium-size liberal arts colleges. After World War II they shifted increasingly to the big university and to the even bigger "research university." The same thing happened in government. And after World War II bigness became an obsession in business. Every firm had to be a "billion-dollar corporation."

In the seventies the tide turned. No longer is it the mark of good government to be bigger. In health care we now assert that whatever can be done outside the hospital better be done elsewhere. Before the seventies, even mildly sick mental patients in the United States were considered to be best off in a mental hospital. Since then, mental patients who are no threat to others have been pushed out of the hospital (not always with good results). We have moved away from the worship of size that characterized the first three quarters of the century and especially the immediate post-World War II period. We are rapidly restructuring and "divesting" big business. We are, especially in the United States, pushing governmental tasks away from the center and toward local government in the country. We are "privatizing" and farming out governmental tasks, especially in the local community, to small outside contractors.

Increasingly, therefore, the question of the right size for a task will become a central one. Is this task best done by a bee, a hummingbird, a mouse, a deer, or an elephant? All of them are needed, but each for a different task and in a different ecology. The right size will increasingly be whatever handles most effectively the information needed for task and function. Where the traditional organization was held together by command and control, the "skeleton" of the information-based organization will be the optimal information system.

From Analysis to Perception

Technology is not nature, but man. It is not about tools; it is about how man works. It is equally about how man lives and how man thinks. There is a saying of Alfred Russel Wallace, the co-discoverer—with Charles Darwin—of the theory of evolution: "Man is the only animal capable of directed and purposeful evolution; he makes tools." But precisely because technology is an extension of man, basic technological change always both expresses our world view and, in turn, changes it.

The computer is in one way the ultimate expression of the analytical, the conceptual world view of a mechanical universe that arose in Denis Papin's time, the late seventeenth century. It rests in the last analysis on the discovery of Papin's contemporary and friend, the philosopher-mathematician Gottfried Leibniz, that all numbers can be expressed "digitally," that is, by 1 and 0. It became possible because of the extension of this analysis beyond numbers to logic in Bertrand Russell and Alfred N. Whitehead's *Principia Mathematica* (published from 1910 through 1913), which showed that any concept can be expressed by 1 and 0 if made unambiguous and into "data."

But while it is the triumph of the analytical and conceptual model that goes back to Papin's own master, René Descartes, the computer also forces us to transcend that model. "Information" itself is indeed analytical and conceptual. But information is the organizing principle of every biological process. Life, modern biology teaches, is embodied in a "genetic code" that is, in programmed information. Indeed, the sole definition of that mysterious reality "life" that does not invoke the supernatural is that it is matter organized by information. And biological process is not analytical. In a mechanical phenomenon the whole is equal to the sum of its parts and therefore capable of being understood by analysis. Biological phenomena are however "wholes." They are different from the sum of their parts. Information is indeed conceptual. But meaning is not; it is perception.

In the world view of the mathematicians and philosophers, which Denis Papin and his contemporaries formulated, perception was "intuition" and either spurious or mystical, elusive, mysterious. Science did not deny its existence (though a good many scientists did). It denied its validity. "Intuition," the analysts asserted, can neither be taught nor trained. Perception, the mechanical world view asserts, is not "serious" but is relegated to the "finer things of life," the things we can do without. We teach "art appreciation" in our schools as indulgence in pleasure. We do not teach art as the rigorous, demanding discipline it is for the artist.

In the biological universe, however, perception is at the center. And it can—indeed it must—be trained and developed. We do not hear "C" "A" "T"; we hear "cat." "C" "A" "T" are "bits," to use the modern idiom; they are analysis. Indeed, the computer cannot do anything that requires meaning unless it goes beyond bits. That is what "expert systems" are about, which attempt to put into the logic of the computer, into an analytical process, the perception of experience that comes from understanding the whole of a task or subject matter.

In fact, we had begun to shift toward perception well before the computer. Almost a century ago, in the 1890s, configuration (Gestalt) psychology first realized that we hear "cat" and not "C" "A" "T." It first realized that we perceive. Since then almost all psychology—whether developmental, behavioral, or clinical—has shifted from analysis to perception. Even post-Freudian "psychoanalysis" is becoming "psychoperception" and attempts to understand the person rather than his or her mechanisms, the "drives." In governmental and business planning we increasingly talk of "scenarios" in which a perception is the starting point. And, of course, any "ecology" is perception rather than analysis. In an ecology, the "whole" has to be seen and understood, and the "parts" exist only in contemplation of the whole.

When some fifty years ago the first American college—Bennington in Vermont—began to teach the doing of art—painting, sculpture, ceramics, playing an instrument—as integral parts of a liberal arts education, it was a brazen, heretical innovation that defied all respectable academic conventions. Today, every American college does this. Forty years ago, the public universally rejected non-objective modern painting. Now the museums and galleries showing the works of modern painters are crowded and their works fetch record prices. What is "modern" about modern painting is that it attempts to present what the painter sees rather than what the viewer sees. It is meaning rather than description.

Three hundred years ago, Descartes said: "I *think* therefore I am." We will now have to say also: "I *see* therefore I am." Since Descartes, the accent has been on the conceptual. Increasingly we will balance the conceptual and the perceptual. Indeed, the new realities with which this book deals are *configurations* and as such call for perception as much as for analysis: the dynamic disequilibrium of the new pluralisms, for instance; the multi-tiered transnational economy and the transnational ecology; the new archetype of the "educated person" that is so badly needed. And this book attempts as much to make us *see* as it attempts to make us *think*.

It took more than a hundred years after Descartes and his contemporary, Galileo, had laid the foundations for the science of the mechanical universe, before Immanuel Kant produced the metaphysics that codified the new world view. His *Kritik der reinen Vernunft* (*Critique of Pure Reason,* 1781) then dominated Western philosophy for more than a century. It defined the meaningful questions even for Kant's adversaries, such as Friedrich Nietzsche. Indeed, Kant still defined "knowledge" even for Ludwig Wittgenstein in the first half of this century. But contemporary philosophers no longer focus on Kant's concerns. They deal with configurations—with signs and symbols, with patterns, with myth, with language. They deal with perception. Thus the shift from the mechanical to the biological universe will eventually require a new philosophical synthesis. Kant might have called it *Einsicht,* or a *Critique of Pure Perception.*

INDEX